Feminist Advocacy

Championing Gender and Social Justice

Jillian Gilchrest, MSW

GREEN HEART
LIVING
— PRESS —

ISBN Paperback: 978-1-954493-75-9

Cover design: Arlene Soto, Intricate Designs

Published by Green Heart Living Press

Contents

Dedication

Dedicated to...

My mom, for telling me I can be anything I want to be.
My dad, for teaching me to respect others.
My brother, for showing me you can manifest your dreams.
My sister, for loving me unconditionally.
My children, for teaching me humility and everyday joy.

To all those who have joined me in the work, thank you. The journey wouldn't have been possible or nearly as much fun without you.

Shannon ... I love you always.

Foreword

A s a member of the United States Congress, I am constantly reminding advocates—whether they are representing a large number of people or simply speaking bravely for themselves—that Congress is an institution that responds to external pressure, and that they—the advocates—are that external pressure. This extends not just to the U.S. Congress but to state government and state representatives, like Jillian, and to local governments, like the New Haven Board of Alders. Our system of government responds to people who put in the work, and who do not give up.

I learned how to advocate from my parents, who committed their lives to helping people, families, and neighborhoods, and making government work for people who are struggling. More than 90 years ago, my late mother, Luisa DeLauro, who was the longest-serving Alder on the New Haven Board of Alders, saw the need for women to engage more in politics and policies.

Writing in a 1933 Ward Newsletter:

"It is not my intention to be critical, rather my motive in writing this article is to encourage the female members of this organization to take a more active part in its affairs. We are not living in the [M]iddle [A]ges when a woman's part in life was merely to serve her master in her home, but we have gradually taken our place in every phase of human endeavor, and even in the here-to-fore stronghold of the male sex: politics. I have noticed that the girls, unlike the men, are timid in asserting themselves, and many a good idea is lost, having been suppressed by its creator. Come on girls, let's make ourselves heard."

While she may have never met my mom, Jillian's experiences and work embody what it means for girls and women to make themselves heard. In this powerful book, Jillian presents her own story and experiences with humility and purpose, posing questions for the reader that helped guide her own self-reflection and growth. The lessons she recounts echo so many of the ones I learned over my career in public service, whether that is understanding the importance of the long game or the bitter but necessary skill of drawing lessons from defeats.

Advocacy is the end of understanding. It can lead to the thrills of victory and the loneliness of losing, but it is always one of the most critical roles individuals can play in our society.

Our democracy works because of advocates like Jillian, and I am confident this book will help inspire even more.

Congresswoman Rosa DeLauro
United States Representative

Introduction

I made it through the final checkpoint. As I placed my hand on the door to the Eisenhower Executive Office Building in Washington, D.C. in 2022, the thought once again crossed my mind, how did I get here? How is it that I—a girl from a small town in New York—am walking into this historic building at the request of the Biden Administration to have a meeting with the president's Gender Policy Council?

For someone who earned her B.A. in Women's Studies, this is both surreal and a dream come true. If you'd told me when I was 10, 20, or 30 years old that my views on abortion would get me an invitation to the White House, I'd have given you quite the look. After all, for much of my life, being a feminist wasn't a badge of honor, as it is for me today. I didn't even understand I was a feminist until college, and in the early 2000s, there certainly weren't t-shirts and posters to welcome that realization. Nevertheless, I have spent my professional life pursuing what would be considered feminist activities and advocacy. From being a sexual assault crisis counselor to advocating for women's health issues, continuing until January of 2019, when I was sworn into office as a State Representative. Today, I am in my third two-year term and proudly serve as the Chair of the Connecticut Legislature's Reproductive Rights Caucus, the Trafficking in Persons Council, and the Endometriosis Working Group.

Even with my background and experience, I have continued to learn things about the legislative process while serving in office. Whenever I'm asked what my favorite thing is about serving in office, without fail I say that it's being in a position to help people translate their experiences into effective public policy. I love learning from people and representing the voices of those in the community. It could be easy to get caught up in politics or to take advantage of the power that such a position grants you, but at the end of the day, I feel grateful for the opportunity. And, I am committed to continuing to listen and learn.

For some people, the idea of becoming an elected official or serving in a position where you can influence public policy might seem unattainable. Yes, there are systemic barriers and individual biases at play that impact an individual's experience and opportunity to lead. For many, their starting line has been unfairly placed behind far too many hurdles. The general assumption is, however, that only a select few get to serve in positions of power. That is not the case. I hope to show you how you can create opportunities, impact your community, and advance feminist advocacy.

Before we begin, I want to acknowledge that my journey to feminist advocacy was influenced by my upbringing, but equally so by what I was and was not taught. I came of age during the 1980s and 1990s in a predominantly white middle class community in New York, and went on to attend the University of Connecticut. My experiences as a heterosexual white girl and woman have influenced my views and shaped my feminism. I have come to understand my white privilege, but recognize that this is an area of growth that I must continuously work at. So, while my journey to feminist advocacy includes this recognition, I cannot and should not attempt to discuss feminism on behalf of Black women, those in the LGBTQIA+ community, or anyone else of a protected class for that matter. My journey is just that—my journey.

What I can do is share my experiences in the hopes that I can help others to be able to do the work they're passionate about. For me, that passion comes in the form of public policy to improve the lives of women and girls. During my more than 20 years of advocacy, I have accumulated some knowledge that I think can be useful as we engage in this next chapter of our country's battle to protect human rights and overcome misogyny.

When invited to speak with students or a group of young advocates, I'm often asked to describe how I got to the position I am in today. In short, it's from lived experiences, and lessons learned. Sometimes they have been really hard lessons. This book is laid out in chronological order, beginning with my childhood, then college, and my early career, and concludes with chapters that go deeper into important lessons learned.

My past experiences and learning opportunities have all led up to where I am today. Thus, the stories shared and lessons learned are meant to illustrate that each of our experiences guides our path and shapes our work. We need more feminist advocates, and it is my hope that this book can support you in that journey.

If there is one constant in our country's history, it's that things are always changing—for better and for worse. Many great leaders have spoken about progress, with the gist being that change takes time and is not linear. Oftentimes when you see gains, those gains are followed by setbacks. I don't like how stark the current setbacks are, but I think there are lessons to be learned from the previous few decades that can help us reclaim the progress we seek and strengthen our resolve for the decades ahead.

During my years of feminist advocacy, I have had my fair share of wins and losses. I've been fortunate to work on public policies that have the potential to change lives, and I've also experienced sexism. I don't come from a political family. I'm driven by passion and a willingness to learn from others. Throughout the last 20 years, I've built lasting friendships with some of Connecticut's strongest human rights advocates. I've learned, cried, and laughed with them. This work can't be done alone, and in order to continue the work, we need others to come along. I hope you will make the decision to join us.

In December of 2022, as I sat across from the Assistant to the President and Director of the White House Gender Policy Council in what once served as the State Department Diplomatic Reception Room in the Eisenhower Executive Building, I felt gratitude. Gratitude for all those I've met along the way who helped me to get where I am today. Gratitude for being able to do the work that I love. And, gratitude for those committed to gender equality. I hope that my experiences can help you in your journey.

Chapter One

Early Experiences

I was born in 1982, the year the Equal Rights Amendment (ERA) was defeated, ten years after Title IX was enacted, and nine years after *Roe v. Wade* was decided by the Supreme Court.[1] Growing up, I never learned about the ERA. Title IX and *Roe v. Wade* seemed like things of the past. Now, having children myself, I can understand how anything that happens before your existence seems ancient. But those events were current and, unbeknownst to me, shaped my experience growing up in the 1980s and 1990s.

We have a habit in this country of teaching only certain history, typically the history of America's white men. We touch on women's history but often just those deemed key figures and landmark moments. When we don't discuss the discrimination, the barriers, and the struggles faced by women to achieve equality, we leave out an important context that shapes the experiences people are living today. In order to move forward, it is imperative that we share our experiences and the experiences of those who came before us.

I grew up in a small town in New York state. I've learned that if you say New York, people assume the city, and if you say upstate, they think Buffalo. We lived in the Hudson Valley, which at the time was fairly rural, and the community in which I attended school was heavily Catholic. I was one of just a few children in my elementary school that didn't attend CCD. My parents had decided to raise my brother, sister, and me without religion. That was fine with me and still is. It just meant that I was different from my friends. Unfortunately, that difference was perceived by them as wrong. It also resulted in my debating abortion as early as the fourth grade.

I'm unsure of how I came to my position on abortion at such a young age. Did I discuss it with my parents? Did I see something on television? I did watch a lot of daytime talk shows. What I do remember is that the debates between my friends and me over abortion got pretty heated. I was staunchly in the camp that women should be able to get abortions and my friends were of the mindset that it was immoral. When I argued that abortion should be legal, making the case that some women get raped, my best friend presented me with "data" to counter my argument telling me that less than one percent of abortions are the result of rape. Reflecting on it now, I'm unsure where she got that statistic, considering these were the days before Google. I remained firm in my position, however, arguing that even if it were just one woman who needed an abortion because of rape, it should remain legal.

It seems absurd that my ten-year-old friends and I were debating abortion, but looking back, we were growing up in the backlash of *Roe v. Wade*. And while it was painful at the time to be on the defensive against my friends, I recognize that they were reflecting what they were being taught in their Catholic upbringing.

Nationally, those who considered themselves pro-choice, but weren't involved in movement work, had just experienced a win. But for those on the anti-choice side, they had just come off a huge loss and were more committed than ever before to making abortion difficult to obtain and illegal. The emotions behind all this trickled down even to kids.

Beyond the absurdity of my ten-year-old friends and I debating abortion, what also strikes me odd is that we were discussing rape. We hadn't even participated in the fifth-grade talk on puberty yet, and there we were, talking about unintended pregnancy and sexual assault. My first impressions of "sex" framed the act as something that can bring women a great deal of shame and something that must be defended against.

"Victim blaming" wasn't a part of the lexicon in the late 1980s and 1990s. We grew up on "stranger danger." I was raised thinking that a van was going to pull up at any moment and some creepy older man was going to pull me in. I didn't quite know what sex was, but I knew that as a girl, bad men might try to hurt me using sex. We were taught ways to prevent an attack or how to avoid an abduction. "Don't talk to strangers." "Be on alert in a dark parking lot." Being armed with this knowledge puts the responsibility on us. When you teach a society of girls and women that they are responsible for preventing sexual assault, and leave out the part where we teach boys not to assault and rape, you make the female to blame when it happens.

No one ever questioned why sexual assaults happened. It was just taught to us as an inevitable reality of our existence. That is the very definition of a "rape culture," a society in which rape is pervasive and normalized due to societal attitudes about gender and sexuality. Despite this, I questioned sexual assault for as long as I can remember. I could never understand why people weren't outraged that men rape girls and women. It seemed to me that we should be doing more to prevent it.

Unfortunately, not enough has changed. Yes, our cultural understanding of sexual assault and "victim blaming" has shifted. And, that is a good thing. But, the way we teach young people about sex is still very much from the perspective of all that can go wrong. Sex education, if taught at all, is often focused on sexually transmitted diseases, unintended pregnancy, and sexual assault. In many schools across the country, students continue to receive abstinence-only education. Some schools now teach about consent, but we continue to live in a society that views male and female sexuality in problematic ways, and that makes women culpable for their own victimization.

I can't recall when I first discussed sex with my parents. I know I asked my mom what oral sex was when I was in middle school because someone mentioned it on the bus. She told me it had to do with water ... Thanks, Mom. I had visions of passionate sex in the ocean for years because of that explanation. When we don't provide people with age-appropriate, medically accurate information they are left to their own devices—figuratively and literally—using their imagination, asking friends, or today, looking it up on the internet.

My father was a physical education and health teacher with a realistic view on sex. He thought it best to provide his high school students, and his children, with accurate information. He was still my dad, though, and as I became a teenager, I was not interested in asking my dad to discuss sex. I actually think I might have blocked out the fact that he was teaching kids my age about sex.

Even with their more progressive parenting style, my parents made it clear that they wanted me to wait until marriage to have sex. I understand their approach and encouragement that sex should be with someone you love and are in a committed relationship with, but the requirement for marriage did place an element of shame on having sex outside of that commitment. It seems to be a holdover from their own Catholic upbringing.

The shame surrounding sex remained a theme as I entered high school in 1996. I went to school in a predominantly Catholic town, and the Board of Education voted on how sex could be taught in our high school health class. The controversy over what could be taught, who could teach it, and for how long, made it clear that sex was a taboo subject and not something we should engage in. The school nurse was given a limited amount of time to come into the class to put a condom on the top of a banana but did not properly demonstrate its use. I remember the condom just sort of sitting there on top of the banana like a hat. It seemed to me that if the condom just sat there at the top of the penis, it could easily fall off during sex.

And, what about the spread of sexually transmitted infections (STIs)? This was the 1990s. The fear of HIV and AIDS was drilled into our heads. Couldn't the uncovered shaft of the penis rubbing against a woman's vagina spread an STI? Clearly, my education was lacking some nuance.

Thankfully, there was a girl on my track team who was two years older than me and involved with Planned Parenthood. One day on the bus, I asked her how the condom stays on the top of the penis during sex, explaining my hat STI theory. She laughed but kindly explained that the condom rolls down over the penis.

I couldn't have been the only one confused by our school's sex education curriculum. I know for sure the basic science of sex was lost on us. By graduation, most of my friends, some already sexually active, had no idea what their periods actually were or what time of month they were most likely to get pregnant.

One of the English teachers in my high school recognized the dangers of how we were being taught sex education and organized for Planned Parenthood to teach us SOS: Safe or Sorry. SOS was a peer mentoring program that taught 20 hours of peer education focused on HIV and pregnancy prevention. My parents signed the permission slip, and I participated in weekly classes off school grounds at the Quaker Meeting House.

I think this was the first time sex was framed as a decision I could make for myself. I was taught about a number of contraceptive methods, making me an active participant in my own sexual health. I felt a sense of control over my sexual future rather than the sensation that sex was something that would happen to me someday. On the final day of the program, we were given a book bag full of protection. I provided the supplies from that book bag to my friends, many of the very ones raised in the Catholic Church who became sexually active toward the end of high school. I brought the remaining condoms with me to college, where I continued to provide friends with the protection they needed.

SOS gave me the tools to ask questions about my sexual health and to make informed decisions. The experience of traveling off school grounds to receive medically accurate information also set the stage for my future activism. I knew the information I was receiving would benefit all of my classmates, but our school wouldn't allow it. The hypocrisy of it all was infuriating. How could people not realize that by prohibiting certain information you weren't preventing behaviors, you were just making people less safe and, in this case, more likely to experience an unintended pregnancy or be pressured to do things they were not prepared to do safely?!

My parents raised me to believe that I could do anything I set my mind to. I just didn't realize that fighting hypocrisy could be a job! I can't recall us ever discussing women's rights or feminism in my household. But, that said, my parents never treated me differently than my brother for being a girl. My dad made a point of teaching me the importance of looking people in the eye and having a firm handshake. It appears they were raising me through a feminist lens without it being overt. When I was auditioning for a school play, my mom suggested I prepare to sing the show's hardest song. She taught me that in order to get what I wanted, I needed to try harder than everyone else. Both of my parents taught me the skills to overcome the limitations of being a woman without harping on the limitations themselves.

During high school, my mom would share how she was limited in her selection of high school sports and career choices. At the time, these stories just confirmed to me that she was old. I didn't view her experiences then, as a child, within the context of the women's movement.

My mom and I are 30 years apart, which isn't very long in terms of culture change. She was just twenty when Title IX passed, and yet her only sports option during high school was cheerleading. I, on the other hand, grew up playing sports, and by high school was competitive in track and field.

As with most policy changes, the impact isn't felt universally. Just because a law like Title IX was passed, it doesn't mean that the culture changes overnight. Culture change is an ongoing process. It is certainly helped by policy change, but culture change must be constantly tended to in order to change individual minds and community practices. While we had a law in place, more subtle forms of sexism were often ignored. While I was fortunate to participate in high school athletics, my town hadn't fully recognized Title IX in practice.

This was seen in the way classes were structured. While I was in high school from 1996 to 2000, the girls' and boys' physical education classes were still held separately. The girls' physical education class was taught differently than the boys' physical education class. For example, only the boys' classes had a floor hockey unit. The girls played badminton.

During my senior year of high school, the PE teacher had the girls class walk the track each class because, according to her, most of the girls didn't like physical activity. As a high school athlete, I found this infuriating and a complete waste of time. I definitely complained to my parents and the teacher, but I only questioned the separate content, not the separate classes.

It wasn't until I was well into my 30s and having a conversation with my dad that he mentioned how the separation of the girls and boys was a violation of Title IX. He said he was always waiting for my high school to get in trouble, but they never did.

While I didn't call myself a feminist back in high school, I was certainly already acting like one! There was the time during high school when my teammates were told they couldn't practice in sports bras, even though the boys were running shirtless. I went to the coaches and called out the hypocrisy. I was successful ... although having the boys put their shirts back on wasn't exactly the result I was going for.

There was also the time that our high school vice principal told the girls they could no longer wear certain tank tops because their bra straps were showing. At the time, those were the popular tank tops that all the stores were selling. I questioned this decision and began asking anyone who would listen why the vice principal was so concerned with our bra strap. I talked to my teachers and coaches, and I told my classmates that it was weird that the vice principal was looking at our bra straps. The whisper campaign about the vice principal looking at our bra straps was enough to shut down the entire debate. He eventually changed his position and we were allowed to wear the tank tops.

I experienced defeats as well, like the time I asked one of my coaches to teach me how to pole vault. I can vividly remember him laughing at me and telling me that girls can't pole vault. While that was his opinion, in reality, the year I graduated high school, women's pole vault became an Olympic sport.

Reflecting back now, I think I was a feminist from a very early age—before I even knew what feminism was. The experiences I had with my Catholic friends early on gave me more than a foundation in debating abortion and a belief in the importance of sex education. It also ingrained in me a contempt for hypocrisy. My friends seemed so judgemental of women when their religion preached to love thy neighbor. As we got older, I watched as they participated in behaviors that they condemned in others, while their religion preached honesty. Hypocrisy was a major motivation for me to speak up.

I suppose at its core, feminism is about overcoming hypocrisy: the hypocrisy of treating women as less than men in a country that claims to value freedom, equality, and justice. My childhood and adolescence were shaped by living in a nearly all-white, Catholic community, while being raised by parents who held the belief that women could do anything, amidst a backlash to the women's movement of the 1960s and 1970s. At the time, though, it was all I knew. No context. No historical understanding of where women had been or where they were going. It would take finding women's studies in college for me to begin to unpack and understand all of that.

Lessons Learned:

- How were issues you care about discussed when you were a child?

- How was sex education taught or not taught to you growing up? How did this contribute to the views you formed on sex and feminism in your early years?

- Did you challenge cultural norms, policies, or practices when you were growing up? If not, why do you think that is? If yes, what did that look like? What lessons did you learn?

- How does it feel to discuss abortion? Are you comfortable sharing your perspective?

1. The ERA was first introduced in Congress in 1923, 75 years after the Seneca Falls Convention. It was introduced every year since, with amended language in 1943, until its passage in 1972. The ERA failed to be ratified by the requisite number of states in 1982. Title IX was signed into law in 1972. Representative Patsy T. Mink of Hawaii, the first woman of color elected to Congress, was the major author and sponsor of the legislation. In *Roe v. Wade*, 410 U.S. 113 (1973), the Supreme Court recognized that the decision whether to continue or end a pregnancy belongs to the individual, not the government. *Roe* held that the specific guarantee of "liberty" in the Fourteenth Amendment of the U.S. Constitution, which protects individual privacy, includes the right to abortion prior to fetal viability.

Chapter Two

Pivotal Moments

Attending college was always an expectation in my family, and my parents generously saved to put my siblings and me through undergrad. I left high school assuming I'd become a famous actress. Besides track and field, school plays and celebrity culture were what I was most passionate about. Since I wasn't going to be running in college, I went to the University of Connecticut to study theater. Soon into the first semester, however, it was clear that I wasn't very good at acting. I also nearly failed my costume design class and realized I could not justify spending my parents' money on learning how to sew, and poorly at that.

From theater studies, I transitioned to communications. During a public speaking course, I watched as my fellow students became debilitated by speaking publicly. It clicked for me that although I wasn't cut out for acting, I was more comfortable than most speaking in public. Today, as an elected official, I speak publicly quite often and, interestingly, I still use the lessons I was taught in that class to help me prepare.

In that course, we were given an assignment to research a job opening and prepare to give a mock interview. I researched sexual assault and discovered that there was a Sexual Assault Crisis Center in Willimantic, Connecticut, about 25 minutes from campus. I hadn't known that such places existed. I was amazed that there were people working to address sexual violence and that these services were available to support women.

For as long as I could remember, I had been horrified that sexual assault exists and baffled that we don't do more to stop it. It both terrified me and angered me that sexual violence was a reality. I was so relieved to see that someone was doing something about this!

After learning about sexual assault crisis centers for that class, I wanted to do more. I reached out to the center to see if I could volunteer. I remember being so nervous that I wasn't skilled enough to participate, but they welcomed me. I participated in their 30-hour crisis counseling training and was certified as a sexual assault crisis counselor. At that time, culturally, sexual assault was still very much thought of as stranger rape—someone jumping out of the bushes. At the crisis center, we used the term "acquaintance" or "date" rape to refer to being sexually assaulted by someone you know. It is common knowledge today that the majority of sexual assaults take place between people who know one another.

But in the early 2000s, we were still trying to give language to the experiences women were having.

During the fall of my sophomore year, 9/11 happened. Before that time, I had never really paid attention to the world outside myself. My community was my friends, and my concerns were limited to which party we'd be attending the following weekend, who was dating who, and how my classes were going. 9/11 changed all that. I wanted to understand who attacked us and why. I paid attention to the news and followed the government's response. During that semester, I was taking my first women's studies, sociology, and anthropology courses to satisfy general education requirements. This was the first time I was taking any sort of class that focused on studying culture and human behavior. The aftermath of 9/11, in combination with what I was learning in my classes, opened my mind and expanded my understanding of the world around me.

I attended my first protest against the war and a rally on campus to hear from Muslim students who were experiencing discrimination. I also had challenging conversations with my friends and family about our government's response and the "othering" of American citizens.

My women's studies classes began to give me a vocabulary for what I had experienced throughout my childhood and what I was living through on campus. It was as if women's studies helped color in a picture that had merely been outlined before. I learned feminist theory, women's history, and the way sexist systems discriminate against women. It was during this time that I learned about Seneca Falls and that the first Women's Convention was held there in 1848, calling for women's suffrage. As a child, my family and I went to Seneca Falls every Thanksgiving to visit relatives for the long weekend. Not once did anyone mention the history that took place there.

I learned just recently that my great uncle helped get the funding and approval for the Women's Rights National Historical Park in Seneca Falls. I've asked my parents why they never shared this history with us or took us to visit the museum when we were kids, and they explained that it just never crossed their minds. I don't judge my parents for not sharing this piece of women's history. It is emblematic of how few people in my generation were raised to think about women's rights.

This is what we do with a variety of topics in U.S. history. We gloss over them—people fought for something and they won. End of story. When we (barely) teach history this way, without context, we don't illustrate how our country's history relates to lived realities today. Maybe that's intentional, maybe it's not. But, by glossing over history in this way, we are stunting our personal and institutional growth and, because history repeats itself and society changes slowly, issues considered settled actually persist. Ultimately, this forces people to live experiences that could have been remedied if we had provided a better understanding of the history that shaped today and enacted true change.

I decided to use my time on campus to gain as much knowledge as possible about the world around me so that I could attempt to change it for the better. I harkened back to my public speaking class and realized that I could use my skills for good—I could speak out about issues of importance. We all bring different skills to the work, and it's the combination and complement of those skills that makes for a stronger movement.

I fell in love with research, and applied for and participated in the Women's Studies Department's academic conference during my junior and senior years. I couldn't believe that I could research things I was passionate about and then have a space to join others and discuss ways to try and change them for the better. While Google took off during my years in college, it wasn't what it is today. For me, being able to use the library's computer database to access research articles on any topic I found interesting was like magic.

During my senior year, I presented research on the cultural misunderstanding and insensitivity of rape. I used our campus's "rape trail" to illustrate my argument. There was a path that led from the main part of campus to two off-campus housing developments where large parties took place. Students referred to this path as the "rape trail" like you would a street name. I was interested in knowing if there were other campuses where students referred to a path by the same name to see if this was a bigger cultural phenomenon than one that was just on our campus. I used my research to argue that referring to a path by something that causes pain and trauma illustrates cultural complacency for sexual assault. I also used my research to correct the misnomer and bring light to the fact that rape on campus was more likely to take place at an off-campus party than on the trail students took back and forth to get there.

Being a white feminist from 2000 to 2004 at the University of Connecticut wasn't looked at too favorably. My experience was most certainly shaped by my almost exclusively socializing with white peers, most of whom came from middle or higher-income backgrounds. It was within this context that on multiple occasions, I would be talking to a guy, only to have him realize what I was and ask in an accusatory voice, "Are you a feminist?" He would then either laugh in my face, walk away abruptly, or tell me I loved killing babies.

I used to defend myself and my feminism by explaining that my main academic focus was sexual violence, not abortion. The abortion debate just felt so toxic. I was also so frustrated that feminism had been distilled down to this one issue—abortion. I thought that if I could show people that there was more to feminism than just arguing about abortion, we'd be able to have a conversation.

I have come to understand that the debate itself is manufactured. The media, politicians, and those opposed to abortion benefit from the toxicity and division that the "abortion debate" brings. They benefit monetarily, politically, and from keeping women quiet who would rather not engage. This division, however, has historically left the experiences of those having abortions out of the discussion allowing people on both sides to debate a hypothetical rather than discuss the realities of women's lives.

I feel fortunate that early in my professional life, I learned that having control over one's reproductive health and body are inextricably linked, and that access to abortion is fundamental to a woman's autonomy. This realization allowed me to push through any discomfort I felt in debating abortion. I have both a responsibility and an opportunity to use my voice to discuss the realities of abortion. Those of us willing to do that are needed now more than ever. But, how do you develop that voice? It took me years of practice to feel comfortable sharing my opinions.

In college, I would grow frustrated when I couldn't get my point across. On more than one occasion, I was brought to tears because I wasn't able to effectively defend my position. We didn't have a debate team in high school, and my family's holiday dinner table language was humor, not hostility. I was completely unequipped to argue my point of view to anyone who disagreed with me.

Beyond the frustration, I also recognized that my tears and exasperation completely invalidated my position. It reduced me to an "emotional woman," making what I had to say not matter because I'd already lost my audience. In my group of college friends, there were a few who absolutely loved to argue. I would observe them as they argued back and forth about anything and everything. What I noticed was that they were arguing to win, not to make their point. And, oftentimes their position would change throughout the argument.

Watching them argue helped me in two very important ways. It solidified for me that I didn't want to argue to win, I wanted to explain my position in a way that people would hear. They also illustrated for me how very important it is to be confident and concise when making your case. This did not come naturally to me. In addition to my struggles with debate, I had yet to share my own thoughts and views at that point in my life, except with those in a class or at a conference who were likely to agree with me.

I had done well academically in high school and was doing great in college, but I was insecure and didn't view myself as intellectually qualified. This would come with time and experience. I've often found myself guided by the mantras, "fake it till you make it," and "act as if," to get me through experiences that have me questioning my ability and preparedness. I also learned a lot by doing.

Early on in my career, I had the opportunity to participate in what was called the Young Women's Leadership Program. It was a steering committee of young women who met to inform the state's Permanent Commission on the

Status of Women. While it can be intimidating at first, by participating in a club, community group, or sorority, you can challenge yourself to step outside of your comfort zone. There were many times in that boardroom where I'd be thinking about something I wanted to share with the group and would freeze, unsure if the point I wanted to make was important or related. What I'd say and how I'd say it would swirl around in my head. Inevitably, someone else would raise their hand and share a very similar idea to what I had thought but was too scared to share. This experience helped me tremendously. It taught me to push through the fear and say what was on my mind.

I'm still the woman who sits toward the front at a conference or in a meeting. I always ask questions and no longer worry if my question is stupid or apologize for asking it. I've heard it said many times over the years that if you have a question, it's likely someone else has the same one, so why not ask it and help yourself and someone else? It's more than okay to ask questions, share your thoughts, and express anger. That's how we learn, grow, and change as individuals and as a culture.

What started out for me as my passion has morphed into a career I never could have imagined but definitely dreamed about. I knew I wanted to use my voice to improve the lives of women and girls, but I never could have imagined the various ways I'm able to do that, and on such a wide range of topics. On any given day I might speak with the press, write an op-ed, post on social media, talk on the floor of the House, or give a speech. I am fortunate that I get to use my voice to shape public policy and inform public discourse, and it is also a responsibility.

I think that oftentimes, people assume other people have it all figured out. They question whether or not they belong or if they're qualified enough to participate. But, the only way to learn is to participate. For a long time, I thought I needed to be good at everything and do it myself, but the longer I've done the work, the more I realize that what's important is recognizing where your strengths lie and the strengths of others. I've been able to use my voice to speak at rallies on a variety of women's health and safety issues. But, if you ask me to create a poster for one of those rallies, I'm at a loss. I can't think of a clever slogan to save my life.

We need one another in this work. Alice Paul described the women's suffrage movement as "a sort of mosaic," where "each of us puts in one little stone." I think that by tapping into our own strengths, rather than comparing ourselves to each other, we can move the work forward in a more effective way.

So, whatever it is you're passionate about or interested in, get involved. Might it be uncomfortable at first? Sure. But it will also likely be really interesting and bring you a great deal of satisfaction. You will find you have strengths you didn't know you had. It can also turn into a career! Seek out the opportunities you desire.

Lessons Learned:

- Do you ever fear that you're not qualified enough for something? What do you do with that fear? How do you overcome it?

- Were there pivotal moments when you were growing up? How did they shape you or influence your understanding of the world and what was happening?

- Do you ever get nervous about sharing your opinion? What are some things you can do to be more comfortable?

Chapter Three

Opportunity & Relationships

M y first job out of college, in the year 2004, was at the Sexual Assault Crisis Center where I had volunteered and then interned during school. If there is a particular organization you're interested in or issue you want to work on, volunteering is a great way to get your foot in the door. Then, when a position opens up, they think of you.

The only position at the crisis center that was open at the time was as a child advocate. I was apprehensive. I was a good listener, which made me a good crisis counselor, but children don't share their thoughts and feelings the same way adults do. I was nervous that I wouldn't be able to effectively help them.

I worked in an area of Connecticut referred to as "the quiet corner" because it is largely rural. But, in our line of work, we claimed it was called that because of the large numbers of individuals who experienced sexual abuse there, but nobody ever heard about it. In my little over a year serving as the non-profit's child advocate, I provided counseling to hundreds of children. I found it hard to turn off the work each day, because I was often troubled by what I was hearing and who I was meeting. I also found it troubling that I, a 22-year-old women's studies major with just 30 hours of crisis counseling training, was the first person—and oftentimes only person—these children were talking to about their abuse.

These children had just experienced a violation so egregious, oftentimes by someone they loved, trusted, and depended on, and I was the only service available to them. At the time, we were the only referral agency available to the Department of Children and Families office in that region of the state. In addition to that, most of the children I met with came from families who didn't have the means to provide for long-term counseling, if those services were even available at all.

I began to grow frustrated, and questioned the lack of services available to children experiencing sexual abuse and their non-offending family members. At the same time, I began to notice patterns. While no two experiences with sexual abuse are the same, men seemed to target single moms with limited means, which created a financial barrier to seeking help when a child disclosed abuse. Poverty in general was a barrier, because often the abuser was the primary source of income for the family. It seemed we could be doing so much more as a society to educate people about sexual abuse and provide survivors with supports and resources.

My work at the crisis center led me to look into public policy. I wasn't cut out for direct service. I'm so appreciative of the people who are. We each play a role on this larger team of creating change. I was interested in working on the social and structural issues that allowed sexual abuse to take place. I wanted to raise awareness and work to prevent sexual violence. To me, public policy was a path to doing that.

I can't recall what I searched for, but I came across the social work program at the University of Connecticut (UConn). Social work is an "academic discipline and practice-based profession concerned with meeting the basic needs of individuals, families, groups, communities, and society as a whole to enhance their individual and collective well-being."[1] At UConn, they divide their master's program into micro and macro social work and offer a focus area in policy practice. I decided to take one class to see if I was interested in the program before matriculating. During that same time, I was hired to serve as a legislative aide and committee clerk at the Connecticut General Assembly. My boyfriend at the time had done an internship at the Connecticut Capitol building, and when the legislative aide for the State Representative he had interned for was leaving, she asked if he wanted to apply for her position. He already had a job, but

I was in the room and said fairly loudly, "I'd like the job." It is moments like those that can change the direction of your life. And, if you don't go for them, someone else will.

I knew nothing about the Connecticut General Assembly or state government in general. I did not come from a political family. My parents voted in every election but we never discussed politics. I went in for the interview and met with three women who would later be my supervisors. The women were all feminist leaders in their own right, and they decided to give me a shot. I quickly realized how unique it was to work for a team of all women at the Connecticut General Assembly and to have been hired for a job in politics with no political experience or connections. I am forever grateful to those women for giving me a chance. I learned on the job, asked a lot of questions, and took every opportunity to learn as much as I could about the process and the people.

Early on during my first legislative session, a group of advocates requested a meeting with the State Representative I was working for. They were part of the Coalition for Choice and were concerned with the availability of emergency contraception to victims of sexual assault at Connecticut emergency departments. I was a legislative aide for the House Chair of the Appropriations Committee. She was a strong feminist leader. Since the Appropriations Committee is responsible for drafting the state budget, she held a great deal of power.

She was unavailable for the meeting, so I asked if I could attend on her behalf. She encouraged me to do so. The statewide sexual assault organization led the discussion, explaining that they had been hearing from their advocates that women weren't uniformly being offered and provided emergency contraception at Connecticut hospitals following a sexual assault. Having just been an advocate for one of their member centers, I was well-versed in what they were talking about. They had been working with the hospitals to remedy this inconsistency. However, as they were having conversations with the state's hospitals about the importance of providing Plan B to victims of sexual assault, the Connecticut Catholic Conference went ahead and established a policy to prohibit any Catholic hospital in the state from offering or providing Plan B to victims of sexual assault.

This is the risk you take in elevating an issue. You risk riling up those who oppose you or disagree with your interpretation of an issue, like the Catholic Conference. So, you need to weigh the impact of doing nothing against the potential backlash for doing something. In this case, sexual assault victims would have continued to fall through the cracks and not be offered Plan B. That was not an option. With the Catholic Conference making it clear that they would ban this practice at their hospitals, the Coalition for Choice knew that the education of the state's hospitals was not enough to remedy the problem. They sought legislation to require that all hospitals in Connecticut, regardless of religious affiliation, offer and provide sexual assault victims with emergency contraception/Plan B.

I was immediately hooked. To me, this was so clearly a victim's rights issue. I had met with women in the hospital following a sexual assault. I had sat by their bedside for hours as they contemplated all of the ramifications of having been sexually assaulted. Pregnancy and potential STIs were chief among those concerns, and Plan B offered at least one morsel of relief.

Victims of sexual assault should be offered all available healthcare—and make no mistake, abortion is healthcare. In a state of crisis, a victim of sexual assault isn't considering whether the hospital they arrived at is affiliated with a religion. They shouldn't lose out on essential preventative care following a sexual assault just because they went into a Catholic hospital emergency department.

I followed the work of the Coalition for Choice that legislative session, but I was so new and so naive. I figured that everyone would see it the way I saw it and the bill would pass. That was not the case.

The first major barrier was that lawmakers and the public lacked knowledge about emergency contraception and the issue immediately became a debate over abortion. As such, the legislation became polarizing. The media covered the division, politicians took their respective sides, and the voices of those impacted remained silenced.

Once again, the lived experiences of women were lost to the "abortion debate." Advocates worked tirelessly to educate people about the difference between Plan B and abortion, but in so doing, most of the conversations surrounding the bill had to do with this distinction rather than rape victims having access to preventative healthcare. Just like in college, the conversation came to a halt when it was made about abortion.

The Archdiocese of Hartford and the Family Institute of Connecticut—an anti-choice advocacy organization—argued that Plan B was understudied and that it terminated a human life.

The FDA had first approved prescription emergency contraception pills in 1998. To claim that Plan B was understudied eight years later was patently untrue. But, the general public and many lawmakers didn't know that. The claim that Plan B terminates a human life is not science; it's a belief. It isn't my place to challenge someone's belief. I just don't want someone's beliefs informing reproductive health policy.

I remember one of my supervisors coming into the Appropriations Committee office suite, turning to me and saying, "They're killing your bill." I went out into the hall in time to see the members of the Coalition for Choice gathered in the atrium of the legislative office building. The bill had been introduced in the Public Health Committee. In order for it to pass into law, it would need to be voted out of that Committee by the committee's deadline.

The Public Health Committee had allowed the bill to be filibustered, which in laypeople's terms means, "talked to death." They called the bill for a vote with 17 minutes left before the committee's 5 o'clock deadline. With all the controversy surrounding the bill, 17 minutes was not enough time for debate, so the committee ran out of time to vote, and the bill died. It would not continue on through the legislative process. It was an election year, and I was told that lawmakers didn't want to have to take an "abortion vote." At the time, the makeup of the legislature was 71% men and 29% women.

That experience put a fire in me. This was common sense legislation meant to protect victims of sexual assault. It was a victim's rights issue and had nothing to do with abortion. Yet, the entirety of the debate that session was about abortion and whether or not Catholic hospitals should have to provide medication they didn't believe in. That's when it clicked. Until women have full control over their own bodies, they don't have any control at all. I thought back to my college experience and how I avoided discussing abortion because of the hostility it arose. I knew that I needed to learn how to use my voice to speak about abortion.

A few weeks after the bill was killed, the Appropriations Committee voted a bipartisan budget out of committee. This meant that both Democrats and Republicans voted for the budget bill. After the vote had been taken, news broke that the Chairs—the legislator I worked for and the Senate Chair—had put language in the back of the budget to require that hospitals provide emergency contraception to rape victims in order to receive financial energy assistance.

A budget is such a large document and typically comes out so close to the vote that most of the lawmakers don't have time to read the language in the back of the budget document before the committee vote. The "back of the budget" language explains how the funds will be used. My supervisor explained that the language the Chairs had included would likely come out and not be included in the final budget that would be voted on by the House and Senate. The Chairs of the Committee had included that language to make a statement.

I cried as I pulled out of the parking garage that day.

I cried because two women, who I'd grown to know and respect, were using their power to push for change. They felt as passionately as I did and they were in a position to do something about it. And, even though they knew that requiring hospitals to offer emergency contraception to rape victims in order to receive energy assistance funding would eventually come out during budget negotiations, they used their power to illustrate just how important it was for victims of rape to be offered and provided emergency contraception in all Connecticut hospitals.

Those two amazing women and leaders continued to use their positions of power to make positive change in the State of Connecticut. The State Representative I worked for went on to serve as Majority Leader and then Connecticut's Secretary of State, and her Senate Co-Chair went on to serve as the first Black female mayor of the city of New Haven. I still get together for coffee with the former Secretary of State and am quick to give a hug when I see the former mayor.

The summer after the bill died, I officially matriculated into the UConn School of Social Work. I selected a field placement that would allow me to work directly with the Coalition for Choice. If you attend a graduate program and are required to do a field placement or internship, push for the experiences that you want. This will help build your knowledge base and give you the professional connections you'll need. In preparation for the next legislative session, the Coalition met to discuss how to message the issue. We discussed what arguments had worked and which had not in year one. That first year, the Coalition's campaign slogan was, "EC in the ER." The group discussed how that message hadn't worked because there was so much confusion and misinformation over what EC (emergency contraception) was.

As the conversation continued, the discussion moved to how the hospitals described the care they provide. We reviewed the hospital websites. The word that kept coming up, over and over, was "compassionate." The Coalition decided that if Connecticut hospitals were truly providing compassionate care, they would be offering emergency contraception. The year two campaign slogan would be, "Compassionate Care for Rape Victims." I absolutely loved the brainstorming that went into talking about the issue, figuring out which legislators to speak to, and deciding who our key messengers should be. We would need to meet people where they were at, which means speaking in ways that are meaningful to them.

While you never want to see your policy defeated, the loss can provide a plethora of lessons that can help you come back stronger in year two. It was clear to me that this is what I wanted to do with my life. I wanted to advocate for policies that would improve the lives of women.

Every state's legislative process is different. In Connecticut, when a bill dies, you have to introduce a new bill the following legislative session, even if the contents of that bill are the same. Legislators are elected to two year terms. The first year is a long session, January-June and the second year is a short session, February-May.

I was able to participate in the entirety of the process, and I loved it. The pre-legislative strategizing sessions were followed by meetings with legislators to build a base of support and answer their questions about the policy. The Coalition planned for the Public Hearing, which is when committee members hear from those who support or oppose the bill.

A committee is required to have a Public Hearing on a bill before they can vote on it.

In planning, the Coalition discussed what key takeaways they'd like legislators and the media to come away with and who best to deliver those messages in their testimony. I learned about vote counting and how imperative it was to have as many members of the Public Health Committee as possible in favor of the bill. Otherwise, it wouldn't make it out of committee again.

Throughout the legislative session, the Coalition for Choice engaged the media by holding press conferences and rallies. This helped to bring statewide attention to the issue and build public awareness and support. Many of the organizations that made up the Coalition for Choice had membership lists of people who they sent emails to. Each organization was tasked with having its members reach out to legislators to ask for their support on the bill. I organized a bus from the UConn School of Social Work to bring students to the Capitol and spoke at my first rally.

I was amazed at the people who were willing to share their personal experiences with sexual assault in the hopes of passing legislation that would protect others from the harm they themselves had experienced. This continues to be one of the most impactful parts of working on public policy. I am always in awe of individuals who, when they experience something terrible in their own lives, respond by doing all that they can to prevent others from experiencing the same thing.

I've been humbled to meet people who have suffered tremendous loss, only to seek changes to domestic violence laws or gun policies. I have worked with an individual who lives with a rare disease and a mother who lost a child to suicide on policies to improve insurance coverage. The people I meet and the experiences they share stay with me and give me strength when the work gets difficult.

In the second year that the bill was introduced, we were successful. Compassionate Care for Rape Victims passed out of Committee, was voted on in the House and Senate, and would be signed into law by the governor. The closest comparison to how it feels to have a policy you care so deeply about getting passed into law is like watching your child succeed at something they love. I was so proud and I felt so much joy.

Soon after the passage of "Compassionate Care for Rape Victims," the executive director of NARAL Pro-Choice Connecticut announced that she would be leaving the position. The organization began conducting a search for a new executive director. I was 25 years old, and although I thought the position was a dream job, I also thought that I was far too young. Who would hire me? So, I didn't go for it.

After months of searching and interviews, however, NARAL announced that they hadn't found the right fit and would be posting the position again. I saw this as a sign, and with the encouragement of my supervisors, I went for it. I researched and printed out nearly 100 possible interview questions. I sat for hours writing out possible responses to those questions and examples of experiences I'd had to illustrate my skills and competencies. I was beyond nervous about the interview, but am a firm believer that you have to fake it until you make it. I went in before a panel of five or six board members, and I nailed it.

I left that night knowing that I had rocked the interview. A few days later I was offered the job, and so at age 25, I became the executive director of a statewide non-profit. My first order of business was to buy a book: *Small Business Kit for Dummies*. I still have the book today as a reminder. I learned so much in that role—most significantly that I needed to be okay with asking for help. This was a lesson I had to learn over and over, unfortunately.

Although we were a statewide nonprofit, I was the only staff member, which gave me a lot of freedom. I think it was a combination of my age and my nature, but I felt like I should be able to handle everything on my own. One person can't handle all things though, and I had to learn how to work with and for a board and how to delegate tasks to interns and volunteers. It took me years to learn to recognize when and where I'm struggling and to ask for help. It took me even longer to realize that doing so is actually a strength.

As the Executive Director of NARAL, I was responsible for managing three distinct entities: a 501(c)(4), 501(c)(3), and Political Action Committee (PAC). The 501(c)(4) and 501(c)(3) distinguish the entity's tax status and its ability to be political. The PAC worked to get pro-choice candidates elected into state office. I met so many interesting people and learned so much about policy and politics. I traveled the state, campaigning for pro-choice candidates, and I got to play a more active role in the Connecticut Coalition for Choice.

I was Executive Director during the 2008 presidential campaign, the first time in our country's history that a Black man was likely to become the Democratic nominee for President of the United States. NARAL Pro-Choice America had endorsed Barack Obama. As a state affiliate, I was invited to attend the Democratic National Convention in Denver, Colorado if I could pay my own way. We were a small statewide non-profit with limited funds, so I purchased my plane ticket and asked a friend's sister if I could crash on her couch. I was 27 years old, had never been to Colorado, and was about to receive a pass to all things feminist at a National Democratic Convention. I would have slept on the floor if it meant attending.

My time in Denver was life-changing. I attended events and heard speeches from Hillary Clinton, Michelle Obama, and Nancy Pelosi. Each state sends delegates to the National Convention who vote for the Presidential nominee. I gave a speech before the Connecticut delegation, following a speech by a family member of the Kennedys. I attended Barack Obama's acceptance speech at Invesco Field.

At some point during the festivities, I saw Fran Drescher. She was at the Convention to lift up the work of her organization, Cancer Schmancer, which educates, motivates, and activates patients into medical consumers, meaning that you are an informed participant in your care. I happened to be in the aisle of the auditorium and she was walking right toward me. I froze but was able to stutter out at her that my mom and I watched *The Nanny* every week together when I was growing up. I thanked her for her work and for giving my mom and I that special time each week. I then walked as fast as I could to the restroom where I proceeded to cry alone in the bathroom stall.

They were happy tears. Tears of disbelief that I, a girl from a small town in New York, had made it to the Democratic National Convention, just feet away from so many feminist leaders I admired. Fran Drescher was my emotional tipping point. She reminded me of evenings spent dancing to the opening number of her television show, dreaming of who I'd become and what I'd do someday. And there I was, listening to, learning from, and advocating with people who believed as I did, that our country could be better for women if we fought hard enough and worked for it. I was able to calm myself down, call my mom and dad, and head back out to the Convention.

At that time, I couldn't have predicted where we would be today on abortion rights. Even though it can feel overwhelming at times, as women across this country die from being denied or fighting to obtain an abortion denied to them, I am driven by my passion and gratitude. It is a passion rooted in calling out hypocrisy in order to make this country a better place for women and girls. And it is gratitude for being in a position to do so, however small or significant my contribution.

Lessons Learned:

- Did you ever go after a job or opportunity that seemed above your qualifications or education? Whether or not you succeeded, what did you learn from the process?

- Are you comfortable asking for help? Why or why not? How can you be more comfortable asking for help?

- Think about an issue that is near and dear to you that you want to advocate for. What kind of language could you craft around the issue to share your stance and encourage others to join you?

1. "Social work," *Wikipedia.com* article. Online at https://en.wikipedia.or
g/wiki/Social_work

Chapter Four

Change Is a Long Game

My decision to leave NARAL Pro-Choice Connecticut was a painful one. As a small non-profit, I was fundraising for my position. The salary was very low for the amount of work that went into the job.

I had my first child while working at NARAL. Before my son arrived, evening board meetings and events weren't a problem. My then-husband was at the beginning of his career and making significantly more money than me. He often had evening meetings as well. Now, with a child at home, nights out meant we had to pay a babysitter.

The amount of money I was making compared to what we were paying for childcare didn't make sense. This led to conflict in our marriage because I felt that the work was worth it, but in the end we made the decision that it would be best for me to look for another position.

I was devastated and felt as though my career was over. I loved the work and feared that I wouldn't find a job that allowed me to advocate for women's health and safety. For me, work wasn't about a paycheck—it was about making a difference. Further, I was living out the reality of so many women in this country.

So often, work that is deemed "women's work," isn't valued by society. We continue to advocate for policies that can address the pay gap between women and men, a gap made worse by race and ethnicity, but jobs in areas such as social work, education, and nursing are still largely held by women, and vastly underpaid as a field at large. This is the baked-in misogyny that is so deeply ingrained in the fabric of our society. Positions typically held by women are paid far less than positions typically held by men, whether it be the same position, or a field as a whole that is largely held by females.

After resigning from NARAL, it took me five months to find a new position. I was fortunate to be hired as an Early Childhood Policy Analyst for another statewide non-profit. I was responsible for engaging those in the childcare industry to understand their needs and frustrations and those of the families they served in order to translate those frustrations into policy recommendations. I had my second child while serving in that position. Beyond the policy work, it was rewarding to learn from those in early childhood while I was raising two young children.

It was during this time that I came across a report from the Center for American Progress about the economic benefits of family and medical leave insurance. I had taken leave with both of my children, and both leaves were unpaid.

I remember thinking how bizarre it was that I was expected not to be paid during a time of increased cost, but I was also just so grateful that I was afforded the time off and guaranteed my job back. In a society that discriminates against women—and unpaid leave for childcare is discriminatory—being given *anything* is appreciated over nothing. Even I couldn't see at the time that this was still inherently sexist.

Change happens when people question the systems themselves. Who were the systems designed for? Who is left out of the systems, by their very design? And then, we must take action to change them. In this case, we have a system that penalizes women who have children. If you are a woman in a position covered by the Family Medical Leave Act (FMLA), you could have your job held for you, but you didn't receive pay. This impacts both your current financial status as well as your future earnings and retirement. And, if you are a woman who works for a position that is not protected by FMLA, then you don't get paid or have your job protected should you need time out of work to care for a newborn. This system was created for and benefits men and businesses.

My then-husband and I could financially afford for me to take unpaid time out of work, but that was not the case for so many individuals and families. As I read the report and did further research, I realized how dire an impact the lack of paid leave was having on individuals and families. On average, women in Connecticut were taking just four weeks off after giving birth. This was problematic for their own health and the health of their children. This is without mentioning that most childcare services didn't accept children until they were at least 12 weeks old.

As I did more research, I learned that there were five states who had systems of paid family and medical leave. Each of them had built off an existing short-term disability program. We didn't have an existing short-term disability program, but that didn't mean it was impossible for a state like Connecticut to pass it, just harder.

I did more research to see if anyone was currently on or had worked to pass a system of paid leave in Connecticut. The state's Permanent Commission on the Status of Women had worked on it, so I knew I'd want to engage them in any efforts moving forward. I also learned that Connecticut had passed a state unpaid Family and Medical Leave Act before Congress, helping to join other states in pushing for federal action. It seemed to me that it was time for Connecticut to lead again, this time on paid leave.

At our next meeting, I asked my boss if I could form a coalition to work on paid family and medical leave. I presented my research and why this issue was important to providing economic security to Connecticut families. He agreed so long as I continued to get the rest of my work done. So, in the fall of 2012, at the age of 30, with an infant and 3-year-old at home, I formed a coalition to push for legislation to establish a task force to study what we then called "family medical leave insurance."

I reached out to a national organization that was working on the issue and quickly learned that maternity leave was not the winning argument. I was told to uplift the other two elements of paid leave—for one's own sickness and to care for an aging or sick loved one. The general sense was that the implicit bias against women is so strong in this country that if we attempted to argue that the policy would benefit women, we'd lose.

I used this knowledge to build a broad-based coalition that included AARP, those focused on chronic diseases, groups interested in promoting breastfeeding, the Alzheimer's Association, and some leading state women's organizations. While it may not be the winning issue, women are the primary caregivers of both children and their aging parents and were the leaders driving the coalition work.

I made a timeline and gave it five years for us to pass the entirety of the policy. The first step was passing a task force that would be charged with studying the issue and reporting back to the legislature with recommendations on how to create and implement the program. We were successful in year one, passing the Task Force bill and bringing attention to an issue that most people at the time thought was a pie in the sky. It ended up taking seven years to pass a system of Paid Family and Medical Leave in the state of Connecticut. Over that time, I left the non-profit I was working for and the Connecticut Women's Education and Legal Fund became the Coalition lead. They worked tirelessly to get the legislation passed. A lot of advocacy, strong leaders, more studies, and the work of so many individuals and organizations helped Connecticut to pass the law in 2019.

Seven years is a long time. When I started the work, my daughter was a baby, and at its passage, she was in first grade. But, in the grand scheme of policy change, seven years is merely a blip. During those seven years, advocates were able to change the culture as they pushed for paid family leave. They built a strong coalition with hundreds of organizations that reached out to the people they serve and the communities they represent to educate them on the importance of paid family leave. Advocates produced reports that illustrated the various benefits of paid family leave. They also hosted numerous community forums to raise awareness and hear the needs of the public.

It can be daunting to have your bill die year after year, but each year you introduce your bill, you are building on the work you did in the previous session. You aren't starting from square one. You are learning from your mistakes, incorporating what you've learned into your arguments, and building your base of support. Each year is progress toward your goal. If you are interested in pursuing policy, you don't necessarily have to be a patient person, but you do need to recognize that change takes time. The beautiful part is that you get to play a part in that change.

In a full-circle moment, I was serving in my first year as State Representative in 2019 and was able to vote "yes" on Connecticut's Paid Family and Leave program. It is remarkable to see something start out as an idea, then blossom into a full-blown movement, and finally become law. I've spoken on the floor of the House a number of times at this point, but getting to stand to speak in favor of Paid Family and Medical Leave will remain a lasting memory. I was beyond proud to vote "yes."

Right before the program officially launched to the public in 2021, I heard an ad for paid family and medical leave on the radio, telling Connecticut residents what it was and how they could apply. I had to pull over the car because I started crying. To this day, seeing the data on just how many people have used the program gives me chills and brings an instant smile to my face.

I left the non-profit that works on early childhood policy for another full-circle opportunity. The Alliance to End Sexual Violence, a statewide coalition of sexual assault victim services programs, was looking for a new Director of Public

Policy and Communications. I would be responsible for advocating for anti-sexual violence policy at the state Capitol and shaping how we speak and think about sexual violence. I sharpened up my interviewing skills once more and went for it. I started my new position in the Fall of 2013. A week later, seven women filed a federal Title IX discrimination complaint against the University of Connecticut alleging the school failed to protect them and afford them their rights after they were sexually assaulted.

The image of those women standing up to a major institution is forever ingrained in my mind. They spoke when others couldn't. They refused to accept a culture that tolerates sexual assault and a system that minimized the impact on victims. They used their experiences to push for change so others wouldn't have to go through what they had. I am forever grateful to them and proud that they challenged our alma mater to do better and be better.

When news broke of the federal complaint, both political parties at the Connecticut General Assembly released statements calling for a full investigation of Connecticut's state university. At the time, as Policy Director at the statewide anti-sexual violence coalition, I knew we needed to act. When you do policy work, you can plan and build your advocacy campaign, like in the cases of Compassionate Care for Rape Victims or Paid Family and Medical Leave, but there are also times when something happens to bring attention to your issue. And, if you don't act, someone else will, and they might not promote legislation that would actually have an impact. This was one of those instances.

I went to my new boss and presented her with the press statements from the state Republicans and Democrats. I told her we needed to make a statement and should ask for a meeting with the appropriate Legislative Committee Chairs to discuss potential legislation for the upcoming 2014 session.

If we didn't act, the legislature would. The University of Connecticut is the state's flagship university. If we didn't provide the legislature with potential policy proposals, legislators would try to pass something into law to address the issues that the students were raising in their complaint. It was imperative that the policy recommendations be victim-centered, not driven by legislators or by the institutions of higher education. This was our policy wheelhouse. We had to be the ones to give them suggestions.

At that first meeting with the Higher Education Committee Chairs, they looked to us for guidance. They didn't know what needed to be done, but they wanted to do something. At the time, the Obama Administration had released a Department of Education 2011 "Dear Colleague Letter" that gave guidance to college campuses on how Title IX related to sexual violence. I looked at that document as I began my research into potential policies for the Connecticut General Assembly to consider.

There wasn't much to go on in terms of state policies, so I began pulling recommendations from campus sexual assault response teams from across the country. I read reports late into the evening, taking notes and categorizing the leading recommendations for best practices from campuses across the country. I created a document that listed a number of recommendations and brought that to my boss to review.

She thought that we might need to limit the recommendations, but I pushed back, arguing that we might as well go in with everything because the legislature was likely to negotiate away some of our proposals. So, we did, and they included every last one of our recommendations in their 2014 legislation. The UConn students who filed the Title IX federal complaint came to the legislature that year to testify on the bill. There was a great deal of news coverage surrounding their case and the legislation. The Co-Chairs of the Higher Education Committee were strong leaders and determined to pass meaningful legislation. And, all four Caucus leaders—the House and Senate Democrats and House and Senate Republicans—as well as the governor wanted to see strong policy passed into law as well.

I can vividly recall being brought in for a meeting between the Co-Chairs of the Higher Education Committee and the representatives from the various public and private institutions of higher education. We gathered in the legislature's largest conference room, and the House Chair told the more than twenty-five people present that they would each be allowed one question. She then said that if they didn't like the answer to the question, too bad. The legislation was happening with or without them.

As they went around the room, the Chair looked to me to answer the questions. At first, I remember thinking I wasn't qualified to be the one talking to these college and university leaders. But, as we went around, I answered their questions, describing the experiences of sexual assault victims and why certain policies were written in a way to address the unique needs of survivors.

They didn't understand why we were requiring all staff to be trained about sexual assault and the various resources on campuses. I explained that if a victim of sexual assault were to disclose, they were likely to do that with someone they felt comfortable with. That might be their residential advisor or a professor or the school's counseling office. In order to avoid the issues being raised in the Title IX complaint, we wanted to ensure that a victim was steered in the right direction no matter who they turned to.

That experience taught me that I was more than qualified to be in that room and I felt so privileged to be in a position to shape public policy. Far too often, we question whether or not we're educated enough or experienced enough. We can let that doubt cloud our knowledge and passion. You are enough. The experiences you've had and the education you've received create your unique perspective, and that's what is needed.

While that is what is needed, society puts up many barriers, particularly for women of color, women with disabilities, and women in the LGBTQIA+ community. Recognition of your value and worth is important, but for far too many, that recognition alone won't open the doors to decision-making. It is incumbent on those of us who hold privilege to make room. Not only is that fair, but it is needed because a diversity of experiences informing public policy moves us closer to the society we need.

We were successful. The bill passed through both the Senate and the House unanimously and was signed into law by the governor. Connecticut's law means that campuses must respond differently to sexual assault and that students are provided with greater education and resources.

I want to stress this again: *policy change and culture change need to go hand in hand.* You need to be working on both at the same time. Just because you pass public policy, that doesn't mean you change public opinion.

This proved true the very next year when lawmakers sought to amend the newly enacted Campus Sexual Assault law to include education on affirmative consent and require schools to use an affirmative consent standard when conducting disciplinary proceedings. Affirmative consent means an active, clear, and voluntary agreement by a person to engage in sexual activity with another person.[1] The year before, many lawmakers voted for the campus sexual assault bill because it was "the right thing to do." The Title IX complaint meant that the system was flawed, but in fixing the system, we didn't necessarily change lawmaker's understanding of sexual assault. Many things, like sexual assault and the roles we assign to men and women, are deeply ingrained in the culture and in individuals.

As an advocate, I met with lawmakers to discuss the bill and answer their questions. Many of those conversations are ingrained in my mind forever. In one instance, I was meeting with an older male lawmaker in his office. Although I cannot remember the conversation verbatim, it went something like this, "But Jillian, let's say there is a young woman who agrees to go on a date with a man. She shows up wearing a low-cut top and a short skirt. Don't you think she knows what's going to happen that night?" To which I responded, "No, Representative, I think she just thinks she looks pretty."

Or, the conversation I had with an older female senator in the hall of the Capitol Building. When I approached her to discuss the bill, she cut me off saying, "Jillian, I have sons!" Her insinuation was that an "affirmative consent" standard somehow made all men culpable for sexual assault. There were a number of people who felt that affirmative consent would somehow make all men rapists. They assumed that scorned women would use this new law to punish a man for a one-night stand they regretted. To that female lawmaker, I replied, "I have a son too, Senator. And I want him to understand what consensual sex is."

As difficult as those conversations can be, they are valuable. Whether it be age, privilege, upbringing or a number of other things, many people have never had these cultural conversations. Providing a safe space to have a difficult conversation is important for both policy change and culture change. In the end, both of those legislators voted in favor of the bill. I don't know if our conversations had anything to do with it, but I'd like to think it may have contributed.

Similar to our experience with Plan B for rape victims, affirmative consent legislation needed more time. While it did ultimately pass, it took two legislative sessions. We learned important lessons that first year that would help shape our advocacy in year two. It was clear that a lot of lawmakers didn't understand the campus disciplinary process that they had passed into law. And, by not understanding the process, they didn't understand that the affirmative consent standard would only apply to those instances where a victim sought recourse through the disciplinary process.

Some lawmakers laughed, accusing the legislation of creating a "hug police," where students could turn each other in for not providing consent. Of course, that was not the case. There was also a lawmaker who made a joke about sexual assault during the public hearing, questioning the legitimacy of affirmative consent legislation because "at the end of the day, there are no witnesses—at least, if there are, it's a really great party."[2]

His joke was disgusting and shocking for the venue, but not at all surprising. When I was in college, my friends would be playing Xbox and one of them would yell loudly at the other, "You raped me." For those who have never experienced sexual assault or for those who don't live in a reality where they are most at risk of experiencing it, there is no sense of the magnitude of what we're talking about. There is no recognition that you are talking about something that changes a woman's life. In using these words casually or by making jokes, there is no sense of the impact that sexual assault has on a person's life.

In year two, we knew that we needed to be more specific about what the policy actually did and that we couldn't assume lawmakers understood what constituted sexual assault and what did not. Year two went better, but it also gave the opposition time to organize. A national group of moms fighting affirmative consent legislation under the guise that it caused young men to be falsely accused came to the legislature to testify against the bill. It was hard to hear legislators discuss how young men's lives were being ruined in the face of concrete evidence that one in four women will be sexually assaulted on campus and most never disclose or receive help.

When preparing for the opposition, I harkened back to the lesson I learned at NARAL about an approach called, "The Group of Three Breakdown." You have to categorize people's positions into three buckets—those who are always with you, those who are never with you, and those who are in the middle. When using this tool it is important not to relegate someone to the "never with you" category unless you truly know that's where they fall. For those who are with you, you want to be sure you're speaking to them using the language you'd like them to use to discuss the policy as well. It will never be perfect, but the more effective you are at discussing the policy, the likelihood increases that they will discuss it in the same way.

For those who are in the middle, which means they haven't thought too much about the issue or are persuaded by both arguments, you want to be sure to meet them where they're at. You need to be able to listen and learn from what they're saying in order to effectively have a conversation with them. Getting defensive or framing your position as obvious is likely to turn people off. The point is to open conversation, not shut it down. As for those opposed to you, while you will likely never sway them, it is important to listen and learn from what they're saying.

Many of us in the advocacy world use a tool called the messaging box.

The messaging box has you consider the following:

- What do **we** say about the issue?

- What do **they** say about the issue?

- What do **we** say about **their** position?

- What do **they** say about **our** position?

Doing this exercise helps you to understand the language the opposition is using to discuss the issue at hand. It is critical to not use the language of the opposition. However, by knowing what they're saying and how they're framing the issue, it allows you to fine-tune your messaging and figure out various ways you may need to discuss the issue to connect with those folks in the middle.

As we were coming to the final days of the legislative session in that second year of pushing affirmative consent legislation, I was invited into one of the leadership offices in the State Capitol with the state senator who was championing the bill. We were asked to have a one-on-one conversation to help the leader better understand the bill so he could explain it to his caucus. As I sat across from this senator and his chief staff member, the staff member became fixated on the bill language that said a past sexual relationship didn't imply consent. I walked him through what was meant, even though in my head I was screaming about how obvious this statement was. There was a moment where I saw the light-bulb go on and he realized that we considered that experience sexual assault. It's moments like those when bringing about policy change *and* culture change finally begin to overlap. This was a moment where someone sees something differently than how they experienced it or were brought up to understand it. Change takes time, but little by little, it can happen.

Lessons Learned:

- Who else can take up your cause with you? (Think of both the obvious partners and think outside the box!) What coalition building can you try?

- Who are the strong leaders in your area? Who are the ones with leadership potential that can be tapped?

- What kind of groundwork is needed (studies, etc.) to get a deeper understanding of the issues important to you? What are the various resources you can look to for research on the policy or issue?

---

1. Public Act 16-106, Connecticut General Statutes.

2. Doyle Murphy, "Connecticut lawmaker: No witness to sex assault party joke," *NY Post*, March 25, 2015. Online at https://www.nydailynews.com/news/politics/connecticut-lawmaker-fire-sex-assault-party-joke-article-1.2162338

Chapter Five

Women in Power

With all the work I've done in gender-based violence and reproductive health, one thing has become clear: white patriarchal society views women as liars. I don't think women lie. In fact, rates of false reporting of sexual assault are consistently very low, ranging from two to ten percent. This is similar to rates of false reports for other crimes.[1] Unfortunately, these misconceptions, driven by stereotypes about women, prevail. No one says, "women lie" that bluntly, but the insinuation is there.

It's a thread that runs across all issue areas impacting women. If the issue is domestic violence, inevitably, I'm told about "the woman" who lied about her abuse in order to get back at her ex. If it's endometriosis, I hear from women who have had doctor after doctor tell them they made up their pain. And, if it's child victims of sex trafficking, I'm told that some of these girls make themselves look older than they are. These beliefs about women, that they lie, are rooted in sexism. They create individual and institutional barriers. At best, it's easier than facing the truth and at worst, it's projection.

It shouldn't be shocking that these stereotypes about women exist, considering our country's history. Our country was founded by white men, for white men. We need only look back at our country's public policies to understand that they were established to protect and promote white men. The right to vote is still the only right guaranteed to women in the constitution. And, it took women 144 years after our country's founding to get that right. From the first utterance that women should be able to vote at the Seneca Falls Women's Convention in 1848, it took 72 years of advocacy—until 1920—for women to get the vote. That knowledge alone is enough for me to acknowledge that our country was founded in sexism. ***Women had to fight for nearly a century to get the right to vote. Are you kidding me?!***

But oftentimes, the mere mention of our country's inherent sexism is met with opposition. "That was then, show me how women aren't equal now?" I've received many comments like this from the disgruntled trolls on my social media pages. In order to understand the sexism we experience today, we must first understand our country's legacy of sex discrimination.

We have done a disservice to both women and men by not teaching the full scope of women's history. In not doing so, we have therefore offered no context to unpack institutional and individual sexism. For example, most people don't know the history of suffrage or the Equal Rights Amendment. Sure, they may have touched on it in a class or two, but when we teach women's history as though it is a singular point in time, it keeps women in the dark and makes them believe their situation is isolated and not part of a collective experience. It allows men to believe it was an issue in the past, now solved. And, it prevents everyone from having a frame of reference within which to understand women's experiences today.

The United States does this with the ways we teach about many disenfranchised groups in American history. While some may argue that this lack of education is simply a consequence of academic time, we are currently bearing witness to public policy choices meant to restrict how students learn about the diversity of experiences. As of 2021, at least eighteen states have imposed bans or restrictions on teaching topics of race and gender[2] and in 2023, four states passed "don't say gay" laws.[3]

The stereotypes and barriers that women face today are compounded for those experiencing intersectionality, such as women of color, those with disabilities, and members of the LGBTQIA+ communities. In discussing our country's history of sexism as it relates to gender-based violence and reproductive health, healthy, cis-presenting white women and marginalized women face different experiences. Women of color, those who don't fit the white cis stereotypes, and those with disabilities, often have a double burden that is inextricably linked to our country's history of slavery, racism, and eugenics.

As I mentioned at the outset of this book, I don't believe I'm the person to speak to this experience. But, I am responsible for working toward an intersectional feminism that recognizes that various forms of oppression harm women of color more. And, I recognize that I am presenting a white-centric perspective on women's history that should be viewed as just that, and not as the only history of women.

Individual beliefs inform public policy and public policy shapes institutions. In order to understand the sexism that women experience today we can unpack the policies that have shaped our current understanding of gender-based violence and reproductive health.

The first mind-blowing realization is that the United States did not recognize marital rape until the late 1970s. This wasn't just some oversight or confusion about how to prove that rape occurred inside of a marriage. State laws explicitly excluded spouses from the definition of rape. What sort of backward view on women does a country have to have in order to declare that, once married, a man has the right to have sex with his wife whenever and however he pleases?!

The history of this primitive viewpoint can be traced back to English common law. It made a woman the property of her father and then her husband. Rape, therefore, was considered a crime of vandalism or tarnishing of a man's property. A husband could never rape what he owned. The historical roots are important to understand because they continue to inform how sexual violence is treated today.

All 50 states didn't make marital rape a crime until 1993. I was eleven in 1993, which means that for the first decade of my life, there were legislators across this country debating whether or not men could rape their wives. According to *Time* magazine, in 1991, when asked about marital rape, an advocate said that the "oft-cited joke about spousal rape—'But if you can't rape your wife, who can you rape?'—no longer described mainstream opinion." But it continued to say that "many people still thought that marital rape was not real abuse but rather 'she has a headache and doesn't want to have sex and she gives in.'"[4] And, there it is again—women lie. She wasn't really raped; she just didn't want to have sex.

We see this narrative pop up time and again in cases of sexual violence. Women are accused of seeking attention, fame, and money when they go public about sexual assault. And, when a man does get convicted, his sentence is often lightened with numerous instances of judges claiming that "he was sorry" or "we don't want this to ruin his life/career/etc." Most often, though, women are simply accused of lying.

After working at the Alliance to End Sexual Violence, I became the senior policy analyst for the state's Permanent

Commission on the Status of Women (PCSW). In this role, I began chairing the legislature's Trafficking in Persons Council. I was responsible for working with a number of partners to make policy recommendations on how to address and prevent sex and labor trafficking. I dug into the laws, trying to understand what we currently had on the books, what was working, and what needed changing.

At that time, if someone was charged with patronizing a prostitute (buying sex) who was under the age of 18, Connecticut law allowed for a mistake of age defense. This means that if a man—and the overwhelming majority of people who buy sex are men—paid to sexually abuse a child, he could argue that he didn't realize she was under the age of 18 and have his charge dropped from a Class C felony to a Class A misdemeanor. In Connecticut, a Class C felony is punishable by one to ten years, while a Class A misdemeanor only amounts to up to one year.

What a bizarre exception. A man could break the law but argue that he didn't mean to break the law as badly as he did, and he could have the charge reduced. What?!

When I challenged this policy and began having conversations with lawmakers, that is when I was met with statements that are inherently sexist like, "Well Jillian, some of these girls make themselves look older than 18." Again, what?! Why does that matter? It shouldn't, but it does because individuals and institutions are sexist. Here we have a child who is being sexually assaulted for money, but it is assumed that this girl tricked an adult man into thinking she was older than she was. She lied ...

At the same time that I was chairing the Trafficking Council, I began working in coalition with a group of organizations to remove firearms when someone is granted a temporary restraining order. At that time, in Connecticut, firearms were removed if someone was granted a full restraining order, but not with a temporary restraining order. Research shows that the most dangerous time for a woman is when she attempts to leave an abusive relationship; if a judge deems her eligible for a temporary restraining order, that means she is in danger.[5]

As we pursued this policy, it became clear that, once again, women were being accused of lying. It seemed that everyone magically knew of some woman who had made up domestic violence to get back at her husband. There were numerous accusations that women would use this provision to take away their husbands' guns as some sort of punishment. Did they miss the part about the women being afraid for their lives? In assuming the worst of women, the fact that hundreds of women die each year in Connecticut at the hands of an intimate partner seemed to have been lost on many people—far too many.

As I mentioned at the outset, this narrative about women seems to be coming from a place of denying reality or projection. There have been many times over the years that I've questioned if women are being accused of lying because the people doing the accusing are themselves liars.

Unfortunately, we need look no further than some of our currently elected leaders to see lies in action. If someone is inclined to lie, then it wouldn't be so far-fetched to assume the same behavior in others. Beyond projection, I think that this "women as liars" narrative has persisted throughout history, shaping our policies and institutions, because the ones leading are men—particularly white men, whose experience and perspective is unlike that of women.

In 2014 and 2017, the #WhyIStayed and #MeToo movements, respectively, brought national attention to how women are treated when they experience domestic violence and sexual assault. These movements are significant and helped move our cultural understanding of sexual and domestic violence. Because of these movements, the terms "gaslighting" and "victim blaming" became a part of the mainstream lexicon. This is important because it gave language to the experiences that far too many women have had.

These movements also helped to unpack the many barriers women face in seeking help, sharing their experiences, and being believed. But, with most things throughout history, these movements faced backlash. #NotAllMen and complaints over "cancel culture" turned the narrative back to white men and their experience.

Having the white male experience dictate policy decisions that impact women's lives is problematic for many reasons and across many issues. You would hope that an elected official can put themselves in someone else's shoes. For example, I don't need to have had cancer to listen and learn from the experiences of someone who has. Unfortunately, there are many lawmakers who can only see things from their perspective—how it would impact them.

When it comes to gender-based violence, particularly sexual assault, domestic violence, and human trafficking, some male lawmakers, see themselves as the accused, simply by default of their gender.

Because these men in power would never commit domestic violence or sexual violence, or maybe because they have purchased sex or have forced themselves on a woman, they approach the public policy from a perspective of how it would impact them if they were the accused. It is, therefore, easier, or serves as a protective posture, to believe women lie, because these men cannot or do not want to see themselves in the position of having committed domestic violence or sexual assault.

Another way we see this "perspective approach" to policymaking present itself is when men speak out against gender-based violence or in support of access to abortion by claiming their role as a father of daughters, a brother to a sister, or the husband to a wife. This frustrates advocates who wish men could just think of women as people, but it illustrates that they are speaking on the issue from their perspective.

While we can certainly change people's understanding of an issue, it's difficult to shift someone's perspective. This is why there is so much research on the importance of women leading. Historically, women lead on different issues than men do and they bring a different perspective.

After years of advocacy it was clear that in order to make significant change, we need women in elected office. Not only do women bring a different lens, but we are also more likely to put ourselves in someone else's shoes. Women bring a different perspective to legislating that is needed. I mean, we've been letting men lead this nation and our states since the country's founding. Maybe it's time to give women a shot. I also grew tired of being told over and over again, "Didn't we do a trafficking bill last year?" Or, "Jillian, we just did a woman's bill." Human trafficking is still happening, and there are a whole host of issues that impact women. We need more women in positions of power to challenge antiquated laws that were created by and for the benefit of men.

So, after hearing this over and over, I decided the time had come. I would run for office.

Lessons Learned:

- What are some examples of institutional sexism you have observed or experienced? What are some examples of individual sexism you have observed or experienced?

- Thinking of the examples you generated in the question above, how would you calmly and logically respond if someone said to you, "That was then—show me how women aren't equal now?"

- Think about your gender identity. If you identify as female or non-binary, what unique perspective does your gender identity help you bring to topics such as sexual assault and abortion?

- If you identify as male, what are ways that you can cultivate empathy for lived experiences you will not have, and how can you elevate female voices who *do* live those experiences?

---

1. https://www.brown.edu/campus-life/health/services/promotion/sexual
   -assault-dating-violence/myths-about-sexual-assault-reports

2. Ileana Najarro, "Many States Are Limiting How Schools Can Teach About Race. Most Voters Disagree," *Education Week*, October 30, 2023. Online at https://www.edweek.org/teaching-learning/many-states-are-limiting-how-schools-can-teach-about-race-most-voters-disagree/2023/10#

3. Samantha LaFrance, "It's Not Just Florida: 4 New 'Don't Say Gay' Laws Passed in 2023," *Pen America*, August 21, 2023. Online at https://pen.org/4-new-dont-say-gay-laws-passed-in-2023/

4. Julie Rothman, "When Spousal Rape First Became a Crime in the U.S.," *Time*, July 18, 2015. Online at https://time.com/3975175/spousal-rape-case-history/

5. "Why Do Victims Stay?" National Coalition Against Domestic Violence's Vision/NCADV. Online at https://ncadv.org/why-do-victims-stay

Chapter Six

If They Can Do It, I Can Do It

From the moment I observed my first committee meeting as a legislative aide and committee clerk, I knew that someday I would run to serve in the state legislature. I firmly believe that in order to reach gender equality, we need to have at least an equal number of women and men serving in elected office. I certainly couldn't tell other women to run for office if I wasn't willing to take my own advice. Plus, I thought I'd be good at it.

I went to many campaign schools over the years. Each of these training sessions was helpful, and gave me the skills and confidence to run for office. If you are considering running for office, and I really hope you are, then I recommend you attend at least one campaign school. There are a number of organizations that host campaign training, and many of those opportunities offer scholarships to help cover the cost. After attending as many trainings as I did, the key ingredients, as I see them, to running for office are:

- Knowing which seat you want to run for and why;

- Building your team;

- Timing.

Like many, I lived much of 2016 horrified. Donald Trump was running for president and making a mockery of our country. I could not believe that a man so vile as he is could be a viable candidate for president. At the time, I was employed as the senior policy director for Connecticut's Permanent Commission on the Status of Women (PCSW), and I wasn't allowed to post anything on my personal social media page that might be construed as partisan. This was a struggle for me, to say the least. How could I not share my concerns about Donald Trump, especially since I viewed my concerns in terms of his blatant misogyny, racism, lying, and cheating rather than as a partisan attack?

That spring, as a result of Connecticut's financial difficulties, the legislature voted to eliminate the state's PCSW. This was a hard blow as an employee of the PCSW, but also for me as someone who had admired the work of the PCSW and what it stood for in Connecticut since the 1970s. As the walls to our office were literally torn down around us, I made a quip to my boss that she and I should finally run for office. Gossip travels fast in the state legislature, and a week or so later, the representative who held the position I might be seeking called me to see if there was any truth to the rumor that I was considering running for office. I let him know that I was interested in the seat but wouldn't run that time around. I asked that we revisit it for the next election.

That call was interesting for a few reasons. First, it was incredibly awkward to tell someone that you are interested in running for the seat that they currently hold. Inherent in that conversation is the belief that they're not doing a good enough job and that you believe you can do better. Second, I was taken aback that he called at all. In the advocacy circles I traveled in, he was notorious for not returning people's calls or taking meetings. I had experienced that firsthand on more than one occasion. I found it telling that he would call me now. And finally, him calling to check on the validity of the rumor helped my inner critic know that the potential of me running was being taken seriously.

After the PCSW was eliminated, I started a new position that allowed me to post about the election. This was a relief, considering that the rest of the 2016 election was a shit show. Along with so many others, I watched in disgust as Donald Trump said and did horrible things.

When the *Access Hollywood* tape was published on October 7th, I thought, finally, that was it. I was driving when that news broke and I pulled over to the side of the road to read the article. As I watched the video of Donald Trump admitting that he uses his power to sexually violate women, I was both enraged and felt a sense of relief. It was finally over. There was no way he could win the presidency now. This would have to be the final straw for the American people. The *Access Hollywood* tape confirmed what we knew to be true from the women who had come forward to share their experiences of being raped, sexually harassed, and assaulted by Donald Trump.

Not only was he capable of such acts, he bragged about them. He is on film saying, "I just start kissing them. It's like a magnet. Just kiss. I don't even wait. And when you're a star, they let you do it. You can do anything. Grab 'em by the pussy. You can do anything."

He described verbatim how men, including himself, use power to sexually violate women and get away with it. His actions were a window into our culture and the dynamics that allow sexual violence to continue at such high rates.

Naively, I believed that seeing this video and hearing his words would be enough for him to lose the election. But just two days later during live questioning at the second presidential debate, Trump dismissed his remarks as "locker room" talk. A man seeking to hold the most powerful position in our country justified his behavior as innocent conversation between men. It was not innocent. His beliefs about women and defense of his behavior exemplify rape culture.

A lot was written on the 2016 Election in terms of how Hillary Clinton was treated. I can't count the number of conversations I had with people who just didn't like her. Whether it be her voice or her attitude or the way the Clintons did politics, I couldn't help but question that if the candidate had been a man, people would have more readily been able to see the stark distinction between that candidate and Donald Trump. For a long while after the election, I wasn't so much disappointed that our country hadn't elected the first female president as I was horrified that a man like Trump had won. I'd love for our country to elect a female president and I firmly believe that day will come, but I'm not surprised we're not there yet. The roots of misogyny are strong, and many individuals' implicit biases against women are so ingrained that, for many people, the role of president is assigned to men, even if that man is patently unqualified.

I, like so many women I've talked to, was in mourning on Wednesday, November 9th. I woke up and went on a run to channel some of my anger before approaching my children who were then seven and four years old. They knew Donald Trump was a bully. They knew Donald Trump had touched women without their consent. They knew Donald Trump was not a good man and that now he had been elected as their president. We had planned to celebrate Hillary Clinton's victory with a Katie Perry kitchen dance party, and now I had to break it to them that sometimes bad people win. We ended up discussing how his presidency meant we'd need to be kinder to people and work harder to improve conditions for people.

The 2016 election of Donald Trump solidified my decision to run for state representative. There was no more time to wait. If a man like that could be elected President of the United States of America, then we absolutely needed more women running and serving in elected office.

In the days following the election, I did what I tend to always do when I'm feeling overwhelmed: I took action. I saw a posting about the Women's March and began reaching out to colleagues and friends to see what was being done to help organize in our state. Soon, I was an active member of the Connecticut Women's March organizing committee. Our main objective was to help get women from Connecticut to the march in Washington.

I took on the role of liaison and began attending weekly video conference meetings with organizers from across the country. I'd then take what I had learned from these national planning meetings and send it to our statewide organizing group. Being able to take my anger over Donald Trump's election and turn it into action was helpful at a time when I felt out of control.

On January 21, the day after the inauguration of Donald Trump, I took one of the many buses that my fellow Connecticut organizers had helped arrange to Washington, D.C. for the Women's March. When we stopped along the way, we saw hundreds of women in pussyhats lined up to use the

bathrooms in the rest area. We arrived at the march late be-
cause of the traffic on the highway leading into Washington,
D.C. The public transportation from the parking lot to the
National Mall was also full of women in pussyhats.

Although we never made it to the stage, we were there—to
stand for the country we believe in and against the type of
man who had been elected. My phone wouldn't work that
day because there were too many people competing for cell
phone service. So, I hadn't been in touch with any friends
or family, except those I was with, and hadn't seen the news.
I am notoriously bad at estimating crowd size, so I had no
sense of how big the Women's March had turned out to be.

When I finally got service, I called my parents. I wanted
them to know I had made it and I was safe. My dad answered
the phone screaming, "You did it, you did it! We've been
watching all day. Millions of women are marching all across
the country and around the world." I still get goosebumps.

The Women's March was the largest single-day protest in
U.S. history. It is estimated that the Washington March drew
over 470,000 people. Between 3,267,134 and 5,246,670
people participated in marches throughout the U.S. That
is approximately 1.0 to 1.6 percent of the U.S. population.
Worldwide participation has been estimated at over seven
million. I do acknowledge that the Women's March would
go on to have many issues as a national organization. However, in its early days, the movement was pivotal in the next
steps I would begin to take.

Donald Trump's first days in office set the tone that we were in for a long four years. I knew he would be awful, but I never could have predicted it would be as bad as it was. I continued to be active with the Connecticut Women's March organizing group, helping to connect newly activated women to already existing advocacy organizations in the state and forming a "Huddle" in my town. The "Huddle" was one of the action steps recommended by the national Women's March group, and it called on women to organize locally.

Our Huddle met monthly until 2020 when the pandemic hit. In many ways, our Huddle reminded me of what I had learned about consciousness-raising groups during second-wave feminism in the 1960s. The meetings were an opportunity for us to share our experiences and learn from one another while discussing important policy and political happenings. The attendance ebbed and flowed, but we always had such fruitful conversations. I built many strong relationships with women of all generations as a result of our Huddle. We took action and we survived the Trump administration together. These women would eventually also help me to run for office.

In addition to the energy I put into organizing for the Women's March and our local Huddle, I began planning my run for state representative. During the fall of 2017, I attended the Women's March Convention in Detroit, where I participated in my fourth and final campaign training. Although I recommend attending a campaign school, four is definitely overkill. I, like many women, experience imposter syndrome, and questioned whether or not I was qualified to run for office. I had been taught, however, about imposter syndrome and the fact that women often need to be asked to run for office multiple times before they do it. Having been taught this information, I was determined to run despite my own imposter syndrome, which apparently manifests itself in overpreparing.

At the convention, Emily's List hosted a training session that hundreds of women attended. It was at that training, more than 650 miles away from home, that I met a young woman who grew up just around the corner from me in Connecticut. The training started with introductions, and we were both shocked to learn that there were two of us in Detroit from our town. She was a senior in college and interested in helping out on a campaign. I was 35 years old and looking to run for office. We met after the session ended, exchanged contact information, and made plans to reconnect during her winter break from school. It would be many months before I'd realize how serendipitous that meeting would be.

That fall, I also met with colleagues I knew from the legislature, people in the community, and members of my community's Democratic Town Committee (DTC) to share my interest in running for state representative. These conversations were a helpful way of making connections, gaining insights about my community, and gathering intel on my potential opponent.

Time and again, the conversation went the same way. I shared my interest in running for state representative. They'd ask who the current state representative was. I'd tell them whose district I lived in. They'd say that although it would be great for him to leave office, there was nothing anyone could do until he decided not to run. While he was seen as a solid Democratic vote, he had served in office for 23 years, and the general consensus was that he didn't respond to his constituents and didn't engage with the DTC. Having experienced his lack of response as an advocate, I found it telling that many people in town had experienced the same as his constituents.

I also learned that there were a number of men who were also interested in the seat and that if he did choose not to run, I would need to get in line, and that I was unlikely to get the DTC endorsement. During that time, I was told that if I was really serious about running I should ask the current state representative to have a conversation. Since we had discussed my interest in running in 2016, I reached out as a follow-up to that conversation. The last thing in the world I wanted to do was meet with him. The phone call was awkward enough, but this time, I asked him to meet in person to let him know that I had every intention of running.

Our meeting didn't go well. He wouldn't say one way or the other if he was seeking re-election, but he made it clear that if he decided not to run, I did not have his support. After the tenor and tone of that conversation, I left knowing that I was going to run for office whether or not he ran.

We have a political primary process in place for a reason. And, if we want more pro-choice, Democrat women in office, which I do, either men currently serving need to step aside and support a woman, or women need to challenge men. Considering that there are many people for whom, once they have power, it can be hard to give it up, the primary process is an important tool for women seeking office.

Some people viewed my challenging a fellow Democrat as an affront, but as we saw with Hillary Clinton, whatever your political acumen, if you're a woman challenging a man for a leadership position, there will be criticism. Knowing that criticism and scrutiny were likely, we did our due diligence to understand how the process works.

In addition to the meetings I had, I also did quite a bit of research to prepare to run for office. I had so many questions. How does one actually challenge someone in a Democratic primary? Did I need to obtain a certain percentage of delegates to get on the ballot? When could I start talking about running for office? How did I qualify for Connecticut's campaign finance program? It seemed the questions were endless and the learning curve steep.

Ultimately, it took me months to research how to run, and every time I thought I found the answer, it came with more questions and confusion. I kept files and took notes. I reached out to lawyers and election officials. I think that in some instances, the information is hard to come by because local parties are led by volunteers and the information is lost with someone's institutional knowledge or to administrative changes. But, in some cases the information is intentionally hard to come by. Those in power want to remain in power, and information is power. It is important that we bring light to the process to make it easier for people, in particular women, to run for office. But until we do, buckle up and start your research early. Ask questions and take a lot of notes.

As a Democrat challenging a 23-year incumbent in a primary election in a heavily Democratic town, I knew I was going to need to build a strong team. I began reaching out to former colleagues, folks I had served with on nonprofit boards, parents of my children's friends I'd befriended, and politically savvy acquaintances and friends. Some people made it clear they could not be public with their support for me but that they'd offer me guidance behind the scenes. I took no offense at all to that.

For many people and professions, relationships are vitally important. If someone wants to help you but requests that help come with certain parameters, evaluate it and decide if it makes sense.

I reconnected with that young woman who I'd met at the Women's March Convention, and we decided working together would be a good fit. She became my first hired staff member and was initially a field organizer. Soon into her work, it became clear she was our campaign manager.

I wanted my campaign to reflect my values, so I was determined to pay my staff as much as I reasonably could and to hire individuals who didn't look like a typical campaign team, i.e., white men. Zippia estimates that over 60 percent of campaign staff are men.[1] I hired all women in their twenties. I knew that, unlike a traditional campaign where the candidate is supposed to be hands-off and let the campaign manager lead, I was going to need to share the knowledge I had gained at the campaign trainings, my experience organizing advocacy campaigns, and my connections to behind the scenes political operatives to inform our campaign team's decision making. This might have been the case at first, but over time, our team of strong young women took ownership and led the way.

Lessons Learned:

- How do you express anger over injustice? How can you take your anger over an issue and turn it into action?

- Did the Trump presidency spur anything in you regarding advocacy? If so, how does that look today? How might it inform future advocacy choices?

---

1. "Campaign Worker Demographics and Statistics in the U.S.," *Zippia - The Career Expert*. Online at https://www.zippia.com/campaign-worker-job s/demographics/

Chapter Seven

Running to Win

I announced my candidacy at a friend's home in January 2018 and raised my qualifying donations in eleven days.

Connecticut has some of the country's strongest campaign finance laws. Our state's Citizen's Election Program (CEP) takes money out of the political equation. Each candidate who participates in the program (and more than 75 percent of candidates do) must raise a qualifying amount of donations from a certain number of individuals in their town. Once the candidate has reached the qualifying amount from the designated number of residents, they qualify for a grant from the state to run for office.

If the program didn't exist, I likely still would have run, but I would have had to contend with the fact that a 23-year incumbent would have had decades of money in the bank and political connections to top donors. Because of Connecticut's CEP, he and I were on equal footing in terms of campaign funding.

During the winter months of 2018, I worked with my team to discuss my messaging and key issues to address in the campaign, reached out to possible vendors, and prepared for the DTC process. I was able to connect with a women-owned print shop that agreed to make my campaign materials. We only had $5,000 to spend because we had not yet qualified for the grant.

While we had raised our money, we needed ballot access in order to qualify. My brother designed my logo and helped me with my website and social media content. Once I had a "walk card" I began door-knocking. I explained to neighbors who I was and why I was running. I'd listen to their concerns and ask for their support. I also reached out to the members of the DTC to ask for their support.

The Democratic Town Committee (like the Republican Town Committee) is responsible for endorsing candidates for state representative and state senate. This is done at a convention, which is like the national process, except much smaller and with no jumbotron. Because I was challenging an incumbent, it was unlikely that the DTC would endorse me, but I was determined to use the process that is in place.

One of the pieces of information that was hard to come by was how I could get on the ballot if I didn't win the endorsement of the DTC. At first, I thought that if I got 15 percent of the votes at the convention then, I would get on the ballot. After multiple conversations with various town and state officials, I learned that I was running in a single-district town, which meant that I had to win the endorsement outright to get on the ballot. If I didn't win the DTC endorsement, then I would need to petition to get onto the ballot.

And so began our research into petitioning to get onto the ballot. We learned that we would need to wait until after the convention to begin the petition process, and then we would have two weeks to obtain all the signatures. We would need to collect signatures from registered, eligible voters equal to one percent of the votes cast at the most recent election for the office I was seeking, or 7,500 signatures, whichever is less. The signatures had to be from registered Democrats, and they had to be on paper, not electronic. We would need to ask people to sign a form with their name, date of birth, address, and signature. There were also rules as to who could obtain the signatures. Anyone who wanted to help get the signatures for the petition would need to also be a registered Democrat and get notarized as a petition circulator.

Once we knew what we needed to do, I was confident we would accomplish it. I've been asked many times since this experience if I thought I would win. I never would have run if I didn't think we would win. At no time during the election did I even consider that we would lose. I always believed we would win the election. That isn't to say that the campaign was emotionally easy. But it does mean that I was running to win.

Despite my inner confidence, there were two times during the campaign when I thought I might vomit and collapse from discomfort. The first was a DTC meeting where I requested to give a speech about my candidacy and ask for their support. This is a typical practice done by candidates for local, state, and statewide office, and I was determined to participate in the process—no matter how awkward. The man I was challenging was in the back of the room as I spoke, pacing back and forth, and there were members of the DTC who didn't look too pleased that I was challenging him. As I've learned to do with my advocacy work, I pushed past the discomfort and my nerves to use my voice to deliver my message. I was later told that it was this speech that got me a vote at the convention.

The second time that I wanted to crawl into a hole was at the convention. At the time of my campaign, I was on the DTC. I knew these people, and some were former colleagues and friends. To sit in a room and have people you know vote against you is hard. It was expected, but it was still hard. In the end, I was successful in getting five of the 23 delegates to vote for me.

The other part of the evening that made it so uncomfortable was the plan we had hatched for after the vote was taken. I knew from my advocacy experience that you can create your own media moments, so I had told our team that as soon as the vote was over, we would all get up and walk into the hallway. They were to surround me with their signs and buttons and I would make a statement. The plan was easier said than done. I was a nervous wreck, but we executed it beautifully. The media followed us out into the hallway for our impromptu press conference.

The next day's news had our photo, and the story was about how we would petition onto the ballot rather than how we'd lost the DTC endorsement. Recognizing that there will be discomfort and learning to push past it is incredibly important if you decide to forge this path.

In order to deal with the emotional hardships of having people who were friends or had been colleagues vote against me publicly or speak ill of me privately, I developed a mantra: "So noted." When someone's actions hurt me, I would say to myself, "So noted." This was the advice given to me by a behind-the-scenes advisor. The process of saying, "So noted" in my head gave some levity to it, but it also allowed me to have a way of recognizing the hurt.

When the campaign was over, this same advisor told me to take that mental list of folks I had noted and discard it. Sure, he said, there might be one or two people who did something so egregious that you can't forgive them, but with all the others, it would be important for me to forgive and move on. And so, that is just what I did.

The petition process was fascinating. At first, we thought going to public events and spaces would be effective, so we got a team of staff and volunteers together and went to the town's Memorial Day parade. The next day, when we went through the petition signatures to see how many we had collected, we discovered that we had to throw most of them out. The majority of people weren't registered Democrats in our district.

I had learned at a campaign training session that standing in front of a grocery store might seem like a good idea, but it's not, because you don't know if the people who are going in and coming out are registered voters. The same was true for the petition process. We immediately changed our plan and began using the voter database to go door to door. We also posted on social media about opportunities for people to come to various locations on certain days and times to sign the petition.

The petition process was arduous, but it was also a wonderful opportunity to meet voters and discuss why I was seeking access to the ballot. There were many people who hadn't made up their minds yet as to who they'd vote for, but they signed because they were supportive of having two candidates on the ballot. Some people were hesitant to share their date of birth or to put their signature on a piece of paper that was being brought around the neighborhood. I wonder if this apprehension has increased since 2018. The process does seem antiquated, and it would benefit from being made electronic.

We collected more signatures than we needed to because we were told that some might be discarded because they were ineligible. After the allotted two weeks to obtain signatures, we were successful! I would officially be on the ballot and receive my grant from the state to run for state representative. This was early June, and the primary election would be held on August 14th. Summer anywhere isn't the best time to run an election, but in the community I was running in, a lot of families take vacations in August. We had our work cut out for us to educate voters about what a primary election is, when it was being held, how they could submit an absentee ballot, and why I was the candidate they should vote for.

One of the people I knew who had run campaigns before but couldn't be public about his support agreed to come to my house and meet with my team. He laid out the game plan—what it would take for me to win. I would need to ID as many, if not all, of the Democrats who were likely to vote in a primary election and then some. ID'ing voters means you figure out who they are planning to vote for by speaking with them. In order to do that I would need to door-knock ... a lot.

And so began my new life. I would work from 8:30 AM to 4:30 PM at my day job, come home to check on the kids and make sure they were set up with childcare, and then head out to door knock from 5 to 8 PM. On the weekends, I would door-knock from 10 AM to 4 PM or 5 PM. By that August, I could play a game with my children where we would drive down various streets in town and I could tell them about the people who lived in each of the houses. I knocked my district eight times over, up until the night before the primary, when I was driven around to specific houses, where I had yet to speak with people.

The campaign got a lot of local media attention. One evening, we had a reporter join us for door-knocking to take pictures and interview people who were willing to go on the record about their support for me. The story was featured in the *Hartford Courant* with a side-by-side picture of my opponent and me speaking to members of the community. I was unable to get endorsements from any of the organizations I had worked with over the years because they had policies of not getting involved in primaries. This was somewhat emotionally challenging, but again, because of Connecticut's CEP, there was no money connected to an endorsement. So noted.

I used social media as a way to connect to voters and bring them along for our campaign journey. We used marketing techniques to make sure that our social media, lawn signs, and campaign materials all looked the same. This meant that everything had the same logo and colors. So, when someone got our walk card, they knew I was the same person they saw on the lawn sign and on social media. There were many times when I would be out door-knocking and someone would tell me that they had seen me on TV. I was not on TV. After the fourth or fifth person said that, I realized that they had been seeing me on Facebook and that our marketing was paying off.

If you've ever worked on a campaign, then you'll know that lawn signs are an interesting part of the strategy conversation. Some people agree with the adage that lawn signs don't vote, but I think that it's important for people to see that other people are doing something that they might be on the fence about—in this case, voting against the incumbent in a Democratic primary. So, part of our strategy was trying to get as many people as possible to agree to take a lawn sign and then, after dark one evening, we had teams of volunteers agree to put the lawn signs out so that in the morning our town was covered with my campaign lawn signs.

The strategy worked, and the buzz around town was noticeable. We also timed it well, because it had the anticipated effect of letting my opponent know we meant business. We were actually told that in those final weeks of the campaign, he had volunteers knocking on the doors of people with my lawn sign to try and convince them to vote otherwise.

The campaign was also a major shift in how I lived my personal and professional life. Up until that point, I had kept my personal life separate from my professional life. Sure, the people I worked with knew I had children and I'd share stories about my life, but I never brought my children to work events or brought my work home to my kids. The campaign changed all of that.

As a grassroots campaign, our headquarters was my dining room table. My team would be in my home when I wasn't. They got to know my children, in particular my daughter, like family. I was apprehensive at first, mostly because I was uncomfortable with blurring those lines. But I really had no choice. I had to embrace the help because I needed it.

I had learned early on in doing advocacy work not to get too emotional or to personalize an issue I was working on. Not mixing the personal with the professional is something I had taken seriously. In politics, it seemed that to do so might make me appear weak, or it might cause the message to lose credibility. I wasn't told this, these are just things I internalized from observing others in the work.

Yet in this instance, I really had no choice. People would be in my home working on my campaign, and there is likely no place where I am more emotionally vulnerable than in my role as a mom. If I let people into my home they would hear me making funny voices, or see me getting frustrated, or experiencing mom guilt. They would witness all of the imperfect messiness of my being a working mom.

If I wanted to win that election, and I did, then I had to let them in, so I did. I was forced to change, which was the most unexpected benefit of running for office. I allowed a group of people to see past the polished me to my vulnerabilities. I worked through emotions in front of people that I would have previously buried or dealt with in private. And in so doing, I have created lifelong friendships for myself and my daughter. I have also learned to be comfortable in being a professional woman with children, bringing them to events which both brings me joy and expands their education and understanding of the world around them. Now, as a tween, my daughter is a stellar networker, and I owe a great deal of that to my running for office. And I feel like I've become a more genuine me.

After months of preparation and hard work, the election day finally arrived. Our team was a machine by that point. We had volunteers scheduled in shifts to hold signs in front of polling places, an activity called "poll standing." We were there all day with our signs at the three voting locations. We also had volunteers at the polls who would relay back who had voted so we could cross-check our voter IDs to determine who we still needed to turn out to vote. I wasn't allowed in my house because my campaign manager didn't want me to see the tremendous amount of work people were doing on my behalf. All day long, my house was filled with volunteers making calls to turn out the vote. The day was filled with many high moments. I had my children by my side as I voted for myself, my parents came to hold signs outside of the polling locations with me, numerous friends volunteered for me, and members of my community shared their support with me as they left the polling location.

When the day came to a close and the clock struck 8 PM, marking the end of the election, I froze. I had been so focused on running for office that I never considered what it would be like if I lost. I turned to the person I was poll standing beside and told him I didn't want to go home. In the nicest way possible he pretty much said, tough, that now all I could do was wait.

My campaign manager had sent everyone to a friend's house down the road where we planned to have the election night celebration. When I came into my house, it was just her and me. I didn't know what to do with myself. All of that work came down to the next few moments. I sat against the wall in my living room with my knees pressed up against my chest.

She didn't want to tell me the results until she was fairly certain of the outcome. We had volunteers at each of the three precincts waiting for the printout who were responsible for relaying the numbers back to her. I ended up missing the call from my opponent as my campaign manager informed me that we had won. It felt like an out-of-body experience, real but not real. When I realized I had missed a call and listened to the voicemail, it was my opponent conceding and congratulating me on my victory. He was gracious.

I won by 150 votes. My campaign manager and I walked, both somewhat stunned, down the street to meet our team, our families, our friends, and our supporters. I called my brother and sister on the way to let them know the outcome, and as we approached the house, some of our team members came running down the street screaming. They knew the outcome but hadn't yet told everyone inside the good news.

We won. Our scrappy team of women and one good man (by that point) had won. For the first time in 23 years, the people in my district would have a new candidate on the ballot for the general election. The feeling in that house as we announced the results is hard to describe, but the looks on my children's faces will stay with me forever. We did it, and you can too.

Lessons Learned:

- Have you ever considered running for office—perhaps even primarying an incumbent? Why or why not? Whether or not you think you'd like to run, how can you support women running?

- Women especially have been taught not to be angry or vocal when upset. In an effort to avoid confrontation or stereotyping as a "bitch", "shrill", etc., many women are more inclined to be quiet. What are some techniques you can use to push past discomfort caused by conflict?

Chapter Eight

The Gentle Lady

Over the course of my professional life, I had walked through the Legislative Office Building hundreds of times, first as a staffer and then as an advocate. But nothing could have prepared me for the immediate shift that took place once I entered as a state representative. Lobbyists who I'd known for years addressed me as I passed them in the halls. The bi-partisan staff called me by my title rather than my name.

As a child, my dad would tell me about how he treated everyone he worked with with the same level of respect, regardless of their position in the school. His words were ever present in my mind as I experienced the sudden shift in power. Everyone plays an important piece in the policy-making puzzle. My new role may come with gravitas, but I'm only able to do the work I do because of everyone else.

As a state representative in my first term, there were many power structures to navigate. After being voted into office by the majority of voters in my community, I now began serving as a "freshman" legislator with many "upper-class" representatives and senators. There was a narrative around the legislature that "freshmen" weren't supposed to speak up. But I had been elected to serve my community, and their support meant I held just as much power as anyone else with the title of State Representative. I respected the knowledge of those who came before me and their work, but I wasn't interested in sitting back. I had two years to effect change, and I was determined to do so.

Having worked as an advocate for so many years lobbying for women's health, safety, and economic security at the state legislature, I had a leg up on understanding the legislative process. I also knew how to bring attention to an issue. During my first session, I wrote op-eds and organized press conferences to raise awareness for the bills I was working on. I could have pulled back and adhered to the "freshman" role, but that isn't why I ran for office. I ran for office because I felt a sense of urgency to pass policies to improve the lives of women and girls and those in my community.

Don't let others dictate the way you're supposed to act or not act. If you have a talent or a skill set, use it.

One of the top issues I was determined to work on as a newly elected state representative was the licensing of nail technicians. State and national research shows that labor trafficking takes place at some nail salons. The exploitation can take a variety of forms, including workers being required to work in a salon all day, but only being paid if they see a client. Some nail salons make workers pay off their training, others house the workers above the salon, and in some instances, the workers aren't paid at all. At the time, Connecticut was the only state in the country that didn't license nail technicians. This meant that our oversight of nail salons was incredibly low, making our state a hotbed for human trafficking. In my role as Chair of the Trafficking in Persons Council, we had been discussing the need to address this issue for many years.

While licensing wasn't seen as the be-all and end-all to solving the issue, it was a policy solution that could reduce the amount of human trafficking taking place in our state. As I began to work on the policy, I also learned that licensing had the potential to legitimize an industry primarily made up of women and to protect public health. I heard from nail technicians who were unable to transfer their skills to other states because they didn't hold a license, and from salon owners who were struggling to compete with the illegitimate salons. I also heard from Connecticut residents who had been harmed at a nail salon and had no recourse. So, not only could this policy potentially protect against victimization, but it could also serve the public health and support a female-dominated workforce.

As an advocate, I was never able to get a bill introduced to license nail technicians because I was told by legislators that the state's Department of Public Health (DPH) didn't like the bill. DPH argued they didn't have the staff they would need to enforce it. This line of reasoning always bothered me considering they were the only department we could work with, and it was their responsibility to license various professions. If they needed more staff to license this profession, then that should be part of the conversation. Now elected, I was determined to work with the DPH to get this bill passed.

I introduced a bill, went to the Chairs of the Public Health Committee, and was shocked when the days kept ticking by and I was unable to get a commitment for a public hearing. In order for a bill to be voted on in a committee, the bill must receive a public hearing. After following up numerous times with staff in the House leadership and the Committee Chair, it was clear that I was not going to have my bill raised in the Public Health Committee.

By this time, having introduced the legislation, I had connected with some women who worked in the industry and who were supportive of the legislation and interested in expanding its scope to include the fields of aesthetics and eyelashes. Connecticut didn't license those professions either. They shared horror stories about treatments gone wrong due to the lack of state licensing. These stories included a woman having her labia torn off while getting waxed and a man who got an infection on his face from an unsanitary facial.

Together, we planned to push for licensing. But first, we needed to get a public hearing. Seeing that I wouldn't get a hearing in the Public Health Committee, I looked for a committee and a bill where I could argue that the topic was germane.

This is where my advocacy experience came in handy. I knew that amendments could be put on bills if they were connected to the underlying topic of the bill. So, I figured that if I could find a bill that had been introduced in another committee and make the case that the licensing of nail technicians and estheticians was relevant to their bill, I could participate in the public hearing and ask the committee to amend the bill to include the licensing provision. I found a bill and discussed the strategy with the women interested in advocating for this policy. By that time, I had also partnered with two other legislators who were interested in the bill.

There are other more nefarious ways to get your bills heard as well. For example, you can threaten the Chair, privately, that you will work against their priority legislation unless they raise your bill. But that's dirty politics. And, long term, if you play a shady game of politics, it catches up with you. You piss off a lot of people and you become known for that. Additionally, as a social worker, I agreed to a code of ethics, which I interpret to mean that I don't use people and policies to get my way.

With that said, I didn't anticipate how my strategy would be perceived. I was just concerned with our concept of licensing getting a public hearing. The majority of lawmakers and the public don't like it when a bill that doesn't get a public hearing gets amended onto legislation later on in the process, so I was determined to have a public conversation about the need for licensing. My strategy ended up making the news, just two months into my first term. This was not what I was looking to do, but it worked. The legislation got attention, and a colleague who I had known since my days as an aide spoke with me about the funding that would be necessary to support this initiative.

My bill concept never made it out of committee, but that didn't hinder me. Change takes time, and you can't let minor setbacks deter you from the larger goal. I continued to work on the policy, meeting with advocates to draft language about how Connecticut could license these professions. I shared the language with the Department of Public Health and went back and forth with a draft bill acting as if it would pass.

Toward the end of the legislative session, I was told that it wouldn't happen after all. There were other policy proposals that would require the Department of Public Health to license two to three new professions, and the scope of nail technician licensing would be too large a population of workers and require too much additional staff. I was advised to amend my bill to be a study and work on the legislation the following year.

But then, with just a few days left in the legislative session, I was called out into the hall to speak with our House Democratic caucus' chief budget negotiator. She shared that the governor's office had agreed to the licensing as part of a bigger negotiation. I went back into the chamber, shocked that this might actually happen after all. They needed policy language to accompany the budget request immediately. Fortunately, I had been working on the language all session and was able to share it. This was my first and most important lesson about serving in office: Always be prepared for what you want to have happen.

Lessons Learned:

- What is a power structure you have run up against? How did you work to change it or go around it? Were you effective? Why do you think that is?

- What are some outside-of-the-box ways you can advocate for issues you care about?

- Think about a time when you made "good trouble"—stepping outside expectations or norms in order to get the job done. What did you do that was effective? What else could you have tried?

Chapter Nine

Abortion Advocacy

With more than 16 years of advocating for access to abortion professionally, not to mention the debates I had in my childhood, I've learned quite a bit. I've learned that having allies in this work who share your passion, make you laugh, and let you cry is essential. I've learned that women's lives are often used as political bargaining chips. And, I've learned that this work doesn't end.

Let's dive into the good, the bad, and the ugly in the hopes that we can use past experiences to inform future debates.

After eight years of President George W. Bush and a Republican administration not favorable to reproductive healthcare, Barack Obama won his election and was sworn into office as president of the United States in January of 2009. As many will recall, one of President Obama's major initiatives was the Affordable Care Act (ACA). In my role at NARAL Pro-Choice Connecticut, I partnered with Planned Parenthood of Southern New England and our national organizations to advocate that the ACA address the medical discrimination women so often experienced in our country.

Before the ACA, the mere fact of being a woman was a pre-existing condition. This meant that women were often denied coverage or faced healthcare coverage that was unaffordable. We pushed to change that and to have maternity coverage, birth control, mammograms, and cervical cancer screenings covered. I traveled to Washington, D.C. with advocates from Connecticut to lobby Congress, meeting with members of the Connecticut delegation in their capitol offices.

The passage of the ACA, otherwise referred to as Obamacare, wasn't the be-all and end-all. There have been many efforts since then that have negatively impacted the goals of the ACA. But, we shouldn't forget what a major step forward the ACA was for women's health and healthcare coverage overall.

The first three jobs I held after college didn't offer me health insurance. As a crisis counselor, I used Planned Parenthood for my healthcare needs, and as a legislative aide and committee clerk, my fiancé and I became "domestic partners" so I could go onto his health insurance. While at NARAL, I attempted to get health insurance for the organization, but I was deemed high-risk since I was of prime childbearing age and the cost to insure me would have sunk the organization's finances. The ACA helped change all of that, and has provided coverage to millions of Americans nationwide.

While we were fighting nationally to have women's reproductive healthcare recognized as healthcare, back in Connecticut there seemed to be a complacency about reproductive rights. Every year, the Connecticut Coalition for Choice would organize a press conference to recognize the anniversary of *Roe v. Wade*. We were lucky to have five people show up.

These attendees were the ones who understood that the rights many took for granted must continue to be fought for, but in large part, it seemed as though many people felt the fight over abortion had been won and was settled. It most certainly was not. The combination of complacency in some people and the preference not to engage in something controversial in others is a major reason we're seeing abortion bans across this country today.

The reason for this is startlingly simple. While it had become easy to be complacent in our current rights, the anti-choice side never stopped moving forward to revoke rights. Even in the years following President Obama's election, there was an increasing number of anti-choice lawmakers being elected to state legislatures across the country. According to the Guttmacher Institute, between 2010 and

2014, 231 state-level abortion restrictions were enacted.[1] While many pro-choice individuals sat on the sidelines, the anti-choice community was using state legislatures to chip away at access to abortion and building a strategy to put anti-choice judges on federal courts.

As we saw with "Compassionate Care for Rape Victims," the anti-choice community used misinformation, judgment, and fear to push their agenda of limiting access to abortion. Some of the restrictions they pushed for included mandatory waiting periods and hospital admitting privileges. Neither of these policies are medically necessary. There is ample research to prove that. But that's because these policies aren't meant to address an issue with abortion care, they're part of the anti-choice strategy. In pushing for these policies, the anti-choice community was able to both restrict access to abortion care and negatively frame the issue.

The anti-choice movement was strategic in how they talked about abortion, framing it as something shameful and dangerous. The policy restrictions they enacted reflected this. Restrictions like mandatory waiting periods before obtaining an abortion called into question a woman's judgment and reason for having an abortion. And, requiring abortion providers to have admitting privileges at a hospital framed the procedure as dangerous when it is anything but. These restrictions made abortions more difficult to obtain, but they also pushed an anti-abortion narrative.

As an advocate, the language we use to discuss issues and policies is strategic. Many organizations contract with consultants to see which messages resonate with the public and how best to frame an issue. This work is done on all sides of an issue. At that time, the language we used in the pro-choice movement was that "preventing unintended pregnancy reduces the need for abortion." It is true that preventing unintended pregnancy does in fact reduce abortions and that providing individuals with information on and access to comprehensive preventative care is important. But, from a messaging standpoint, the language we used was problematic and played into the anti-abortion movement's framing of abortion as shameful and dangerous.

If you want to reduce the need for something, doesn't that inherently make it objectionable? This messaging harkens back to language that was used by Bill Clinton in 1992 when he called for abortion to be safe, legal, and rare. Once again, if you're calling for something to be rare, you seem to be buying into the anti-choice messaging that abortion is wrong. It is an important lesson across any policy issue that you be firm in your own position rather than react to the position of your opposition. While there were other factors at play, I think that the years of pro-choice defensiveness and abortion shame contributed to the climate that ultimately led to the overturning of *Roe*.

For instance, when I was running the NARAL Pro-Choice Connecticut's PAC, which endorsed pro-choice candidates and worked to get them elected into the State Legislature, it was common for a pro-choice candidate to ask that their support for abortion not be made public. Sure, they accepted our endorsement, but they made it clear that abortion wasn't something they wanted to run on. They'd rather avoid the topic.

Throughout the 2000s, the Democratic Party also struggled to take a firm pro-choice position. Every four years, both national parties create a platform of values meant to guide the political party. The Democratic platform has long supported abortion, while the Republican Party has not. But, the language the Democrats have included in their platform has changed over time. The 2004 party platform included the language "safe, legal, and rare." That changed in 2008 when the Democratic Party shifted to a stronger stance, stating that the Democrats unequivocally supported *Roe v. Wade* and "a woman's right to choose a safe and legal abortion." (This was the language used then, however now we would say something like "an individual of child-bearing potential.")

Interestingly though, the 2008 platform also included language about reducing the need for abortion. This language remained until the 2020 platform, which includes the Democratic Party's strongest position on abortion to date. Even with the party platform as their guiding principle, the Democrats continued to support anti-choice candidates.

In 2017, the Democratic Congressional Campaign Committee (DCCC) provided financial support to an anti-choice Democrat. They defended this choice, with then-Committee Chair, Representative Ben Ray Lujan of New Mexico, arguing that he would not impose a "litmus test" on candidates and that the Democratic Party was a big tent. I joined other pro-choice advocates in Connecticut at the time to condemn the DCCC's support. Abortion is a personal decision but when it comes to public policy or a political position, we need leaders who will recognize that their personal views shouldn't be imposed on others. We also need a party that will stand strong—especially if they include it in their platform. You can personally be opposed to abortion and still support policies that protect access to abortion care.

Oftentimes, someone's personal views are tied to their religious upbringing or current faith. I'm not asking anyone to forgo their beliefs, but I am asking them not to push their beliefs on others.

A political candidate is seeking to represent a diversity of people. It is incumbent on those of us in the Democratic Party to speak with our colleagues or would-be candidates who are personally struggling with abortion and help them to think through how they can hold their own personal views and recognize that when it comes to public policy, we need to ensure that people have access to the care they need—care that includes abortion.

Unfortunately, there are many people who don't consider the multitude of reasons why an individual has an abortion, let alone consider it healthcare. Maybe one of the consequences of the decades-long debate over abortion is that people think about abortion in terms of sides—those who are for it and those who are against it. The media certainly has portrayed the issue in this manner. And, we can see how this polarizing thinking influences the legislature. In 2019, advocates began efforts to pass legislation to address deceptive advertising at crisis pregnancy centers but because of legislative pushback and the pandemic, the bill wouldn't be signed into law until 2021.

By way of brief history, crisis pregnancy centers (CPCs) came out of the anti-choice movement. The first crisis pregnancy center in the United States opened in Hawaii in 1967 after that state legalized abortion. In 1968, the first network of centers was established by Birthright, closely followed by Heartbeat International, and then Care Net, a network established by the Christian Action Council. There are currently more crisis pregnancy centers in the U.S. than there are abortion providers.

The strategy of CPCs is and has always been to dissuade women from having an abortion. They do this in various ways. Prior to passing legislation, pro-choice advocates in Connecticut documented CPCs that had their staff dress like medical providers to make women think that they were at a health clinic, tell women abortion causes cancer—which is untrue—and give women medically unnecessary sonograms just to show them pictures of the unborn fetus. There was one Connecticut CPC that changed its name from the St. Gerard's Center for Life to the Hartford Women's Center and located itself just 20 feet from Hartford GYN, an abortion provider, to confuse women seeking abortion care.

Thus, during the legislative debate in Connecticut over CPCs, the CPCs portrayed themselves as a community resource and argued that they were being unfairly targeted because of their views on abortion. This simply was not the case. The CPC legislation was intended to address the fact that CPCs were lying to women seeking reproductive healthcare in the state of Connecticut. Their views on abortion were irrelevant. It is true that some of the CPCs in Connecticut provide new moms with baby bottles, diapers, and other supplies. But, it is also true that CPCs lie to women as a well-documented strategy of the anti-choice movement. If a Connecticut CPC was not lying to women, then this legislation wouldn't apply to them.

This is where that notion of "sides" comes into play. It didn't seem to matter to certain legislators, who viewed this policy as an attack on CPCs by the "pro-abortion side." Rather than see this legislation as an attempt to ensure that women in Connecticut receive medically accurate information, some lawmakers viewed it strictly from the lens of one side vs. another. In addition, the years of anti-choice misinformation and framing of abortion as something shameful and dangerous had lawmakers questioning what was or was not deceptive.

I had the privilege of taking the bill out on the floor of the House. I was serving as the Vice Chair of the Public Health Committee, and had championed the legislation through the committee process. The Chair offered me the opportunity to lead the debate on the bill, and I jumped at the chance. In the days leading up to the floor debate, I was told that it could last a long time. In the Connecticut General Assembly, the Democrats hold power in both the House, Senate, and Governor's seat, which means that the Republicans' greatest power is time. They can debate a bill for hours, winding down the clock until the end of the legislative session.

The Speaker of the House had planned on the CPC bill being a "talker", so it went earlier in the session, but still, he gave me a heads up that he was anticipating that the debate could last six hours. In actuality, I stood on the floor of the House and debated the CPC bill for a little over eight hours. I'd do it all over again in a heartbeat if it means even one woman isn't lied to seeking reproductive healthcare in the state of Connecticut. Over the course of those eight hours, a lot of intense things were said. Misinformation was spoken, and bizarre questions were asked. But, I remained calm, I answered each question succinctly and honestly, and I learned quite a bit.

I learned that you need only answer the question asked. Sometimes a legislator would talk for quite a while about their opposition, making statements of complete misinformation. I had the impulse to correct what they said, but then they'd change direction, and by the time they asked a question, it would seem odd for me to return to a point they had raised minutes before. I had to get comfortable with the fact that I had already stated the facts. They were out there and I had to let them stand. Throughout the debate, I had my colleagues available to me via text. I had done my research and had notes prepared, but if something came up that didn't make sense or I was uncertain about, I knew that the advocates were there to send me information or support.

After that marathon debate, the bill passed. There are moments you don't forget. I won't forget that feeling of accomplishment. Believing in something so deeply—in this case, that women shouldn't be lied to when seeking reproductive healthcare—preparing diligently, debating rigorously, and then succeeding. We passed a law that honors women's autonomy and provides them recourse should an entity attempt to misinform and confuse them.

Since its passage, the law has successfully held up to a lawsuit. Connecticut was the first state in the country to ban deceptive advertising at CPCs, and we are sharing our experiences with those in other states with the hopes that they will pass similar legislation.

We are doing a lot of that these days—sharing legislation amongst states where abortion remains legal. As I write this, we are seeing the aftermath of *Dobbs* and the overturning of *Roe*.

Every week, I read a story or am sent a news link about an individual whose life has been negatively impacted by being denied access to abortion. There are women who are being denied healthcare when they present at a hospital with an ectopic pregnancy, or some other pregnancy-related medical issue, because providers are fearful of violating an anti-abortion state law. There was the child who was raped, became pregnant, and was unable to access an abortion in her state. And in Texas, there was a woman who was murdered by her abusive ex-partner after getting an abortion out-of-state in an attempt to sever ties with him.

Those of us working to protect and expand access to reproductive healthcare which includes abortion aren't doing it because we are on a "side." We are doing it because we understand that everyone's experience is unique and that having access to abortion care is vitally important. I think what frustrates me most is, once again, the hypocrisy. The "side" in favor of access to abortion recognizes and responds to reality. The "side" against it does not and as a result, women are dying. Again, I'm reminded of my childhood debates over abortion and my high school's (lack of) sex education. My Catholic friends attempted to push their beliefs on me, even though their actions didn't reflect those beliefs. That's how a post-*Dobbs* America feels. Christian fundamentalists are pushing their views on abortion on everyone, including those of other faiths. Meanwhile, those of us on the "other side" are giving light to the lived experiences of those capable of becoming pregnant.

There are obviously advocacy groups working to protect access to abortion and those working to restrict it. But unlike those working to restrict access to abortion, those working to protect access aren't pushing any particular "side" on people. They are trying to ensure that people can access the healthcare they need, whatever care they deem appropriate for themselves.

It became clear to me that *Roe* would be overturned when the Supreme Court allowed a Texas law to go into effect. That law banned abortion after six weeks and deputized citizens to turn people in who they believed assisted someone in getting an abortion. The Supreme Court allowed this law to go into effect before issuing their decision in *Dobbs*, which sent a message that they were likely not going to protect *Roe*. Recognizing this, I partnered with a colleague to form the Reproductive Rights Caucus during the 2022 legislative session. Our caucus strategized legislation that could protect Connecticut against Texas's law, and potential copycat legislation, and expand access to abortion in the event that *Roe* was overturned.

Connecticut led the way with the passage of the Reproductive Freedom Defense Act to protect providers and individuals who provide or assist someone from another state in obtaining an abortion in Connecticut. We also expanded the types of providers who could perform abortion care in Connecticut. While there were legislators who voted against the bill, the climate had shifted in the spring of 2022, and many people understood the urgency to take action to protect access to abortion care. Our legislation passed right around the time that the *Dobbs* decision was leaked, giving us and the entire world a heads up on the mindset of the Supreme Court and where they were headed in terms of access to abortion care. And as we might have guessed, their ultimate, published opinion is laced with misogyny and reeks of Christian fundamentalism.

In the aftermath of the *Dobbs* decision, we must do all we can to protect individuals seeking reproductive healthcare in this country. Women's lives are in danger as reproductive healthcare is becoming increasingly limited based on legislation that restricts how OB-GYNs can perform care. We also have an opportunity to reflect on how we have advocated for access to abortion since *Roe* was decided in 1973. This must include an examination of how we discuss abortion, what types of abortions society deems acceptable, and why so many people felt such a sense of complacency after *Roe* was decided.

Almost immediately after *Roe* was decided, the Hyde Amendment was signed into law, prohibiting federal funds from being spent on abortion care. For decades, people accepted the argument that taxpayer dollars shouldn't be spent on abortion, further removing it from under the umbrella of healthcare. In practice, the Hyde Amendment created barriers for low-income individuals and women of color seeking abortion care, a policy that remains in place today. If we believe that abortion care is healthcare, then everyone should have access to that care free from restrictions.

Another restriction that remains a significant point of contention is "parental consent" or "notification" for a minor to obtain an abortion. At first thought, many people have the reaction that parents have a right to know what their children are doing. The good news is that most children do speak with their parents about healthcare decisions. But there are children who don't have that relationship with a parent or for whom their parent is the very person hurting them. We need to ensure that these children have access to abortion care, free from restrictions.

What would it be like to get to a place where there were no restrictions to access abortion care? The United Nations, in using a human rights framework, regularly calls for governments to decriminalize abortion in all cases and to ensure access to safe, legal abortion.[2]

We must reject any framing that stigmatizes abortion. Abortion is a viable healthcare option—period, end of sentence. This may seem a hard line to take because we are so accustomed to caveats. How often have we heard someone say, "I'm pro-choice, but..."? As we are seeing in the aftermath of the *Dobbs* decision, "exceptions" to abortion bans for victims of sexual assault or to protect the health of a woman are simply restrictions. In practice, these policies don't allow someone to access care. We can and should look to other countries that don't view abortion the same way we do. They recognize unique experiences that individuals have and trust women to make the decision that is best for them.

Abortion care should be viewed on the continuum of reproductive and sexual health care. While we have traditionally separated out abortions, we are now seeing in practice how abortion bans are impacting access to the full range of reproductive healthcare. Women in states that have imposed restrictions experience higher rates of unintended pregnancy and maternal and infant mortality, with women of color and low-income women disproportionately impacted.

Finally, we must push back on this notion of "religious freedom." The anti-choice community has also been strategic in their co-opting of "religious freedom." Most recently, they used this argument to strip rights away from the LGBTQIA+ community in the Supreme Court's June 2023 decision to allow a website designer to discriminate against a gay couple seeking a wedding website. They're not arguing for religious freedom—they are fighting to have their particular religious beliefs pushed on the rest of us. This is evidenced by the simple fact that other major religions, such as Jewish and Muslim faiths, do not strive to outlaw abortion—for themselves or for others.

We must lead the discussion on abortion, not respond to it. We can't allow the media and politicians to frame abortion as a two-sided argument when it is a vital part of reproductive healthcare. And, we need to challenge the misogyny that puts women on the defensive by judging us and our decision-making.

Ultimately, the "debate" over abortion is a red herring. A truly "pro-life" society would end poverty, make housing more affordable, increase access to healthcare, and invest in childcare—but those same "pro-life" advocates vote against all of these things, time and time again. The anti-abortion movement is about controlling women's lives and pushing Christian fundamentalism. We can never grow complacent again.

Trust women. Believe providers.

Lessons Learned:

- How do you talk about the issues you care about? Are you using the lens of those in support or those in opposition? What would happen if you used a different lens?

- How do you prepare for something you've never done before, like testifying during a public hearing, bringing a concern to a superior, or even debating a bill on the floor of the House?

- If you are attempting to educate or debate someone whose religious beliefs are the foundation of their worldview, what kind of wording and tactics could you choose to better be heard?

---

1. Heather D. Boonstra and Elizabeth Nash, "A Surge of State Abortion Restrictions Puts Providers-and the Women They Serve-in the Crosshairs," *Guttmacher Policy Review,* Volume 17, Issue 1, March 1, 2014. Online at https://www.guttmacher.org/gpr/2014/03/surge-state-abortion-restrictions-puts-providers-and-women-they-serve-crosshairs

2. "Q&A: Access to Abortion is a Human Right," *Human Rights Watch*, June 24, 2022. Online at https://www.hrw.org/news/2022/06/24/qa-access-abortion-human-right

Chapter Ten

Lessons From When You Lose

I have learned that legislation is usually defeated for one of two reasons. First, either good intentions are misguided or miss critical foundational needs of the very community we hope to help. Second, sometimes the issue is so big and the opposition so loud that you can't break through the noise (at least not yet).

Prior to serving as a legislator, I had learned another important lesson that I brought with me into my work as a State Representative: listen to the communities you seek to help.

I learned this lesson after making mistakes early on. Before understanding this, my approach was to reach out to various organizations with a policy idea, tell them how it would help the communities they serve, and ask for their support. This didn't work very well because I didn't start with listening.

I hadn't built trust with the people I was trying to serve. I was an outsider coming and telling a community what they needed. Also, sometimes the policy I was coming to them with, while important, wasn't the pressing issue for those I was trying to help. An example of this was my advocacy work with paid leave. Early on, we were looking to build support for the policy by engaging various constituencies across the state. The research on paid leave was clear that this policy would improve conditions for low-income families, in particular women in Black and Brown communities. I identified a community-based organization of mothers in New Haven, Connecticut, and reached out to see if I could present at one of their meetings, and they agreed.

When I went in to talk about the paid leave policy, it was clear that they faced far more pressing issues. They were worried about paying their electric bills. They were worried about the poor quality of education their children were receiving. They were worried about putting food on the table and keeping a roof over their heads. The here and now—that's what mattered. Rather than going in and telling this group of women what would benefit them, I should have gone in to listen to what they were experiencing. In addition, I was powerfully reminded of my first week with the Connecticut Coalition Against Domestic Violence, when I shadowed my colleagues on a Monday morning court visit. Monday mornings are the busiest time at the criminal court for domestic violence cases because many incidents take place over the weekend. The first woman we met was a young mom who looked pregnant. She held a child on her lap. Her husband had beaten her and was in jail awaiting arraignment. The purpose of our visit was to let her know what services were available to her. She listened to my colleague, but when she finished, this woman was most concerned with when her husband was able to come home. I was stunned. He had hurt her and she wanted to know when he would come home. As my colleague continued to speak with her, she shared that her husband helps with childcare and that until he could come home, she would not be able to work. They would be losing much-needed income. Despite the fact that it was a dangerous situation, her immediate day-to-day needs were most pressing. In order for us to help her, we would need to meet those needs first—and then turn to empower her to escape the dangerous situation at hand.

These lessons would carry me forward in the legislature. A major issue I wanted to work on during my first session in office was gun violence prevention. I came to the issue of gun violence prevention like many white women of my generation and demographic. For me, it was after the mass shooting in a movie theater in Aurora, Colorado. I couldn't understand how someone who appeared to have severe mental health issues was able to access an AR-15. A shooting like that in a movie theater brought an element of fear to everyday activities. And then, just five months later, the massacre of children in an elementary school in Newtown, Connecticut happened.

I, like so many, sat horrified by what took place in a Connecticut elementary school. I was supervising an MSW student through her field work at the time. She had grown up in Hartford, Connecticut. As we discussed the mass shooting in Newtown and the trauma that those families and children were experiencing, she shared that she too was a victim of gun violence. Her brother had been killed at a sleepover (in a break-in), and her high school boyfriend had been shot in front of her in retaliation and had become a paraplegic.

That's when it clicked. The trauma that those who are victimized by mass shootings experience is felt by those in our urban centers on a daily basis. That new feeling of fear to participate in an everyday activity was something those living in neighboring communities had felt their entire lives.

That realization, and my understanding that policy work must be driven by the communities you seek to serve, motivated me to want to learn from those who were doing the work to address community gun violence.

During my first session as a state representative, I met with various groups in Hartford and New Haven to get a sense of the work they do and how they seek to prevent and address gun violence. I attended vigils, walked in marches, and visited community-based organizations to get a better understanding of the work and the need.

It became clear from my various meetings that one of the biggest needs was funding. These organizations knew what works. They had established effective programming to address community gun violence, but they were woefully underfunded. After meeting with these various groups, I pulled research from the Giffords Law Center and Everytown for Gun Safety and found that the interventions these organizations were using in their programming were part of a comprehensive community-based violence intervention strategy—street outreach, group violence intervention, and hospital-based violence intervention.

The issue in our state isn't that we don't have these interventions, it's that we aren't funding the interventions at the levels needed. So, I met with the groups again and pitched the idea of establishing a designated funding stream to support these programs. And, the way we would pay for it would be through a tax on ammunition. As I would soon learn, unfortunately, my approach to this proposal wasn't well thought out.

The Second Amendment was never meant to allow for the abundance of guns in civilian hands that we find ourselves with today, nor did it allow for the evolution of the simple guns of yesterday into the mass-killing machines of today. Guns are making American society less safe, and they make it harder for law enforcement to do their job. Recent statistics show that firearms are the leading cause of death for children in the United States, and when a firearm is present, victims of domestic violence are in more danger, not less.[1]

With these factors in mind, I went big with a proposed 50% tax on ammunition. And, my proposal was met with a big reaction. I should have anticipated the blowback from my proposal, which was viewed by Second Amendment supporters as a double-edged sword—anti-gun and a tax. I spent that first session playing defense instead of discussing the importance of funding these programs.

I learned from my mistake and introduced a modified bill the following year, which received a public hearing. While the intent of the legislation is good—to bring in revenue for community-based violence intervention programming, this proposal is a multi-year endeavor. I needed to engage more colleagues in the legislature and advocates in the field.

The pro-gun lobby in Connecticut is small but vocal. They show up, they call, and they email. Unfortunately, with a lot of policy proposals, we hear more from those who are opposed to the legislation than those who are in favor of it. Those in favor don't often feel compelled to express their support. This is problematic because it gives a false sense of how big the pushback is to a particular policy, and because it emboldens those opposed to the legislation because they are the only ones making noise.

Going forward, I need to build support amongst my colleagues who might be apprehensive about a piece of legislation that receives such strong pushback from such a vocal minority. The way we talk about this policy is also important. Rather than it being framed as something punitive toward gun owners, we need to discuss it as an investment in preventing gun violence.

In the midst of working through the backlash for the ammunition tax, one of the community groups that I had met with to learn from approached me with a policy that they were interested in working on. This policy would support their efforts to prevent and address gun violence. Hartford Communities That Care had been providing hospital-based violence intervention services for decades in the city of Hartford, and had recently expanded its efforts by forming a collaborative to help partners across the state offer these services to other cities. They were interested in having Medicaid cover some of their hospital-based violence intervention services. Medicaid is the state's health insurance program for some low-income individuals.

Having worked on the licensing of nail technicians legislation and from serving as a subcommittee Chair on our state's Medicaid oversight committee, I knew that in order for a service or provider to be eligible for Medicaid, the work needs to be recognized by state statute. That was as far as my knowledge on the subject went, but I also knew who the key players were at the Departments of Public Health and Social Services. This was at the start of my second term in office, and I was serving as Vice Chair on the Public Health Committee.

I spoke with the Chair about having the bill raised and got a commitment that we would receive a public hearing.

The collaborative that formed to support the effort was amazing. These were people who had experienced gun violence or the loss of a loved one to gun violence and were motivated to prevent others from experiencing what they had. There were emergency room physicians who treated victims of gun violence and a national organization dedicated to the hospital-based violence intervention model. I learned so much from them about their work and its value, and I helped them to better understand the legislative process. I told them what to expect at the public hearing and the types of information that would be important for committee members to hear.

On the day of the hearing, they had a number of individuals who were prepared to speak. They did a fantastic job of explaining the scope of their work, its impact on the community, and the need to receive sustainable funding.

We were able to pass a bipartisan bill out of committee and then through the House and the Senate to define the work of hospital-based violence intervention professionals. This set the stage for the second phase of the work—Medicaid reimbursement of these services. The bill also charged the Department of Social Services (DSS) with planning for this reimbursement.

In the weeks and months following the bill's passage, members of the collaborative and I met with DSS to talk through what coverage would look like. I met with members of the governor's staff to ensure alignment on our goals of having these services reimbursed by Medicaid. Passing legislation is as important as ensuring it gets implemented. I'm grateful for the relationships I've been able to establish with those in the executive branch who are responsible for enacting the legislation that we in the legislative branch pass.

After months of conversations and planning, DSS submitted a Medicaid state plan amendment to the federal government that was accepted. Connecticut became the first state in the nation to have hospital-based violence intervention services reimbursed through Medicaid. This work never would have happened without the voices of those most impacted. Listening and learning from those in the community is critical to enacting effective public policy.

I continue to take these lessons with me to the present day, most recently with a policy I've spent three years working on pertaining to consent in criminal sexual assault law. Currently, our criminal law is very much focused on force and resistance, and we have been trying to pass legislation that would establish a new criminal charge of "sexual assault in the absence of consent." We have hit several barriers to this proposal that seem unlikely to change in the near future. My coalition of advocates requested that we focus on other more pressing needs right now and re-visit this policy in the future. While it is extremely difficult for me to let go of this proposal at this time, I recognize that if they believe we need to use their time and energy differently, then I accept that. I will follow their lead, and simply ask, "How can I help?"

I believe that we will come back to this issue in the future and be successful. Recognizing that helps. We can still use this time to lay the groundwork, have conversations, and continue to build support. It's a long game—and even though we have shifted our attention from legislation, the work that leads to change will continue.

If you want to be an effective advocate, you have to show up for other people before they're going to show up for you and the issues you may be advocating for. And sometimes, when you meet people where they are at, you discover that while you are passionate about an issue, sometimes that issue isn't what a community needs at that moment in time. You may have to let it go ... for now.

Lessons Learned:

- Have you met with members of the community most impacted by the issue you're working on? Where can you go to find those people?

- How can you show up for others before they show up for you?

- Have you ever reached out to your elected officials to let them know you support something they're doing? Why or why not? (If you haven't, take some time right now to identify who your elected officials are and write down their contact information!)

---

1. Bailey K. Roberts, MD; Colleen P. Nofi, DO; Emma Cornell, MPH; Sandeep Kapoor, MD, MS-HPPL; Laura Harrison, MPH; Chethan Sathya, MD, MSc, "Trends and Disparities in Firearm Deaths Among Children," *Pediatrics* (2023) 152 (3): e2023061296. Online at https://doi.org/10.1542/peds.2023-061296

Chapter Eleven

Sexism at Work

Throughout my career, I've had many people shake their heads in disbelief, thank me profusely, or exclaim that they could never do the work I do. Reactions like these always strike me as funny, because they usually come from someone who does a job that blows my mind, like a teacher, nurse, or cancer researcher—professions that I am in awe of.

We each have an important role to play, and I couldn't do what I do without the knowledge that so many people impart to me. I just so happen to be passionate about public policy and love strategizing the types of advocacy that can help to bring about change. But, I only know what change needs to happen because of the people I meet and the things that I'm privileged to learn from them.

Obviously, though, this role is wrapped up in politics. And, considering that "politics" is often cited as something so socially toxic that you should never discuss it at a family gathering, I can understand why people are shocked that I've chosen to actively participate in it.

For me, the "politics" pales in comparison to the misogyny and sexism I have experienced over the years. When it comes to politics, I understand the power dynamics and the egos. I recognize that information is currency and that your word and your reputation are inextricably linked. And, for as much as I dislike it, I realize that bills can become collateral damage when a legislator feels slighted.

As much as I know that I'm working in a still largely male-dominated field and I'm likely to experience some form of misogyny, oftentimes, when it happens, I am caught off guard. I hate to think that when discussing my work as an advocate and elected official I need to share this aspect, but it is a reality. Over the years, when I have met with young women who are interested in learning about my career path, they inevitably ask about how I've experienced being a woman in politics. I'm truthful, but I don't often share the specifics of my experiences. I do that both to protect them and myself.

I've decided to do so in this book because I want you to be prepared. I certainly don't want you to live each day expecting the worst, but as much as we've worked on preventing and addressing sexual harassment, it still happens because sexism and misogyny are still very much present. (I am able to reflect back now that, as an elected official in my 40s, I am known as a feminist leader.) I am no longer an easy target.

What follows is the truth I wish I had known, the things I wish I had been better prepared to respond to. If I had known such behavior presents itself in such very unexpected ways and times, maybe I wouldn't have been so blindsided.

It's hard to revisit some of these experiences because when I do, I realize just how messed up they are. In many ways, it's easier to ignore them, to focus on the positive, and to provide a playbook for how to follow your passion. But, the path to your passion will likely include misogyny, and it isn't fair to gloss over that reality. I don't think that in sharing these experiences I'll be able to help make anything you experience less jarring, but I do hope that I can share some of the tools I've used to work through them.

I experienced my first shocking event when I was just starting out as a legislative aide and committee clerk. Being so new to the legislative process, I was in awe of watching the state senators and representatives debate. Listening to the legislators during committee meetings and on the floor of the House was fascinating to me. There was one legislator in particular who was so funny in the way that he delivered his opposition. Even though I disagreed with his positions, I was always impressed and often entertained when he spoke.

On the final night of the legislative session, they used to have a large party that ran from late at night into the early morning. There is still a rendition of the "end-of-session party." It might have gotten tamer, or maybe I just don't stay as late. It's hard to say. At age 24, though, I was enjoying myself.

That year, the "end-of-session party" was taking place all across the Capitol building. At one point in the evening, I saw that legislator who had made such an impression on me. I decided to walk up to him to tell him how much I loved watching him debate. Without skipping a beat he responded to me by saying, "I'd fuck you so hard your head would pop off." I screamed, abruptly turned away from him, and ran across the third floor of the Capitol building. I can still hear the clicking of my heels as I fled from him.

He was double my age at the time, and a legislator. I gave him a compliment, not an invitation for sex. I shared the experience with some of my closest friends who validated how completely inappropriate his comment was. We also got a good laugh out of it considering how bizarre his comment was. Does that line really work on some women? I ended up telling a close colleague what had happened because I was horrified to see him again and was still questioning if I had done something wrong. She validated me by assuring me he was indeed in the wrong, something I still needed to hear.

I've thought a lot about my reaction that night. Not surprising but still infuriating, I questioned if my comments made him think I was flirting. Here I was, young but already a feminist advocate, and my first thought was still reflective of the rape culture and patriarchal society I had grown up in. As evolved as my thinking had become, and as much as

I championed women's issues, I was not immune to that innate and ingrained reaction at first.

In the end, talking to those closest to me was as far as I took it. There had been drinking involved, and he held political power. That combination was a recipe for disaster. He'd made a comment, albeit violent and disgusting, but nothing had happened. This was the mid-2000s, before #TimesUp and #MeToo. I wasn't about to potentially ruin my reputation and career in order to question his. It's hard to say if I'd react differently today. I'd like to think I would. Certainly, in the position I'm in now, I hold more power and would say something.

We've also been able to make much-needed changes to how sexual harassment and violence can be reported at the legislature. I'm proud that during my first year in office, I worked with staff to improve the response to sexual harassment at the capitol. We now have an anonymous option available to staff. So, if that were to happen to a 24-year-old me now, I might feel safer reporting it. I always regretted that by not reporting he might have done something similar to someone else, or worse.

I've recognized over the years that I'm quick to minimize how sexism and misogyny impact me. As someone who works to address gender-based discrimination, harassment, and violence, I know this is absurd. It is the complete opposite of how I would react to anyone else who experiences something similar. I think I react this way because I know that my experience pales in comparison to the women I've met and learned about over the years. I also recognize how fortunate I am to be in my position and to have the support that I have. That said, I do have a reaction. And, rather than compare my experience and minimize it, it is important for me to process it.

For me, having an outlet to share my experiences has allowed me to process, let go, and move forward in the work. I'm grateful that I recognize that today and can connect with people who can help me talk it through, even if it takes me a while. For me, this looks like talking with other advocates who do the work. They understand my passion in ways others might not. And, it's as simple as taking a walk together and, quite frankly, bitching about what's going on, what was said, or how frustrated you are. Developing those relationships along the way is as important to you as it is to them. When all is said and done, I think the negative experiences themselves are less important than understanding the need to process what you experience.

Over the years, I've experienced many gender microaggressions. When I was first running for state representative, a well-known radio personality on our local NPR station referred to me as "some young woman." I was 36 with two kids and an established career. And at one point during the Crisis Pregnancy Center (CPC) debate, around hour six or seven, one of my male Republican colleagues walked across the well of the House, looked up at me, made eye contact, and said, "Smile."

I had been standing much of the day, microphone in hand, listening intently as my Republican colleagues questioned and criticized legislation meant to ensure that women could access reproductive healthcare without being deceived. I remained calm minute after minute, hour after hour, as my colleagues chose to ignore a reality in which women are harassed for trying to access abortion and abortion providers have been killed.

I had spent the entire day remaining respectful and composed as my colleagues ignored the history of CPCs and the anti-abortion movement in this country. And now, as we neared seven hours of debate, a man told me to smile. I don't know what expression came across my face. Apparently I can't keep a poker face in all circumstances. I do remember letting out an exasperated laugh and I might have rolled my eyes.

The majority of women have been told to "smile" by some man at some point in their life. As with all the other times it's been said to me in my life, I was ripped from my concentration. After my laugh/eye roll/half smile, I stood there dumbfounded. How far ingrained must the sexism be for a man to not even question telling a state representative in the middle of a debate on the floor of the House of Representatives to smile?

Other than my initial shock, I didn't make anything of it. I completed the debate, the bill passed, and it was signed into law. There is no point in making enemies in the legislature. I did, however, share that interaction with close friends and family who I feel comfortable venting with.

Creating outlets to share your frustrations is vitally important to the work. For me, I love to read romance novels, take dog walks, run on the treadmill, and zone out to reality TV shows. I encourage you to proactively find your own outlets to process and decompress. We need you in this work long-term, so it is important to figure out ways to take care of yourself.

Then there are situations where I feel like I'm crawling out of my skin while listening to a public hearing or a committee meeting. Like the time I was lobbying for affirmative consent and was told that girls with short skirts should expect to be raped. I learned early on that if I get upset or show too much anger, or god forbid cry, my message is lost. At best, I become just another "emotional woman." At worst, I'm an "angry feminist."

Once again, having outlets to share these experiences has been key, as has humor. The topics I work on can be intense, and those of us working in this policy arena often turn to humor to cope. Maybe we make jokes to keep from crying, but in my experience, having people I can turn to and laugh with about the absurdity of it all is vitally helpful and keeps me going.

I'm glad that I developed these tools throughout my time as an advocate because I never could have anticipated the level of sexual misogyny and vitriol I would receive once elected to the legislature. It started out as mild, but quickly gained steam.

When I introduced the ammunition tax during my first session in the legislature I shared a video about the proposal via what was then known as Twitter, now the company X. That tweet was shared by the NRA, and soon I was inundated on all of my social media platforms by haters from across the country. Not surprisingly, the majority of these white male haters went after my looks, in particular the size of my forehead. I had always thought I had a big forehead. In fact, I'd had bangs my whole childhood because of it. There was this moment when I first read the comments where I was like, 'Oh wow, okay, so other people do notice that I have a large forehead.' And then, I just sort of laughed.

It struck me as hilarious that these angry men were proving my point with every comment they made. When they told me to go back to the kitchen or they questioned who would ever want to fuck me, they were demonstrating the misogyny that persists throughout our society. I was certainly overwhelmed by the volume of hate I was receiving, but I also felt vindicated. For so long, I had been beating the drum of sexism, and here it was being directed at me just because I introduced a bill that some men disagreed with.

Unfortunately, I've grown accustomed to the daily trolls on my social media pages, and it does impact how I would prefer to interact with my constituents. It's unfortunate, because I used to use my social media pages to engage my constituents. Now, I only post—I never reply. There is no point in responding to comments, because the trolls are relentless in their desire to oppose anything I do or say.

After drawing their attention with my position on guns, there are certain men who won't leave my page. They comment on every post I make no matter how mundane. One dude is obsessed with calling me a man. To others, I'm a baby killer. Most times, the stupidity of their comments makes me laugh but then at other times, I am shocked by the pure level of evil some will sink to!

A couple of years ago, near the end of my first term in office, this came into disturbingly sharp focus. There I was, going about my day, and I impulsively opened Facebook and clicked on notifications. I saw that I was tagged in something, specifically a photo, and clicked to open it. And then, I was in it. I was torn away from whatever it was I was doing and was thrown into the middle of a most bizarre crisis.

The image was of my head, but my head was on some other woman's body and I was sitting on a couch with four large Black men hovering above me. The governor had been superimposed into the photo as well and he was standing to the side of the couch holding something. I could not comprehend what I was looking at. I knew it wasn't good, but I was so confused. I began to get a panicky feeling.

I decided to screenshot the image and share it with some close friends to better understand if my reaction was similar to their reaction. As time passed, it became clear that I had been photoshopped into an image from a porn movie in which Black men "run a train" on a white woman. To "run a train" means multiple men have sex with a woman, one after the other, with or without her consent.

This image was shared by a board member of a Connecticut group that pushes a Second Amendment agenda. Not only was the picture sexist and potentially depicting sexual violence—considering the something the superimposed governor was holding was a large fist that said, "Do Not Lube," but the picture was also portraying a racist trope of white women being sexually violated by Black men.

I couldn't let that stand. I couldn't sit by and let someone who argues for greater access to guns share that image without being called out. I made an official statement and called on my House leadership to also make a statement. I also notified the governor's office and the police. There are some instances where what is said or done is so egregious that you can't simply let it go. In situations like this, it is important to use it as an opportunity to take back the narrative.

My statement addressed the increasing violence in political rhetoric, how Black men and women are disproportionately victims of gun violence, and that sexual violence is not something to be joked about. My statement was picked up by the media, and the non-profit that this man was a board member of was pressured to make a statement and condemn the image. In that instance, it was important to bring attention to a social media post in order to make a larger point about societal ills.

Since getting elected, I've had to contact the police at least seven times. I've sort of lost track. The first instance was when a man contacted me via email to tell me I had to "hook him up" with a victim of trafficking or he would hurt himself or someone else. I sat frozen staring at my computer screen, filled with fear, and questioning what I should do. He had made a threat to hurt himself or someone else. Once again, I contacted some trusted colleagues who recommended I call the police.

It was with this experience that I learned that when you are threatened or harassed via the web, the police will come to your home to take a statement from you. This is impor-tant to know, because if you have children or a partner, you might want to reconsider and meet at the station to make the report. In that instance, the police went to the man's home and he was charged with breach of peace.

In addition to the image mentioned above, I've had to call the police about a man from Massachusetts who wouldn't stop calling me to harass me about the nail licensing bill, and about a man from California who posted on Facebook that it would be a shame if I were shot in my big forehead. Neither of those instances rose to the level of a threat, so nothing could be done.

We need to look at how we address behaviors that are red flags for potential violence against women. Current law is still heavily reliant on the presence of an active threat of violence and a plan to enact that violence. But, if we can see that someone's behaviors are escalating, we should intervene before the violence is imminent and then takes place.

Current policy and practices are rooted in systemic misogyny and have been enacted by and for men for far too long. So, even when a man is exhibiting signs of mental distress that could lead to violence against himself or someone else, public policies, in large part, prevent any interference. By default, this protects the aggressor and not the victim. We are beginning to see more "red flag" laws that allow law enforcement to step in and make referrals for mental health treatment, but we need more of that. Men have had their chance to fix this, and they have done nothing about it. It is my belief that we need more women in office in order to pass laws that can prevent violence against women.

Even when a threat is made, that too isn't always enough for law enforcement to do anything. During my second term in the legislature, as we were working to pass the Reproductive Freedom Defense Act, I received a death threat at my home. Once again, there I was going about my day when all of a sudden I was thrown into a crisis involving myself.

I was opening the mail, and there it was, a letter threatening that if I passed a bill on abortion I would be killed. I stood frozen in my dining room. I actually put the letter down and walked into the other room, as if by leaving it I could ignore what had just happened. But, I couldn't, and so I returned to the letter and called my legislative aide, who told me I had to call the police immediately. It's weird to need outside validation in these instances to understand that the situation is serious when I am often the one providing that validation to others.

I went to the Capitol Police and my local law enforcement to report the death threat. I also took to social media to address the hypocrisy of a "pro-life" group threatening death for my position on abortion and to call for civility in political discourse. Unfortunately, the police were unable to determine who or where the letter came from.

While the entire experience was scary and frustrating, I think the worst of it might have been when one of the officers I reported it to said, "Well, Representative Gilchrest, we choose the issues we work on." And there it was—misogyny out loud from one whose only role should have been to protect. Victim blaming is common and we must call it out because no, it shouldn't matter what issue I work on. I, and no one else, should ever be threatened with death for their political or policy views.

These experiences are intense, but I don't share them as a way of scaring you off. I share them to encourage you to establish your toolkit for taking care of yourself. Figure out who those key confidants are and what brings you joy and relaxation. As best you can, don't take it personally. See the sexism and vitriol for what it is: symptoms of misogyny.

I've used my experiences to inform and fuel my advocacy. I know why women don't tell. I know that we need more women in office. And, I know that as an elected official, I have a responsibility to serve as a role model and pass legislation that can improve conditions so that someday this chapter will be a story from the past, and not a preparation for what women are still just as likely to face tomorrow.

Lessons Learned:

- How do you process negative things that happen to you? What can you do to expand your toolbox of coping skills?

- Who are the people you can laugh with when things get tough?

- Think about microaggressions you may have experienced. How did you respond then? How might you respond now?

Chapter Twelve

Once an Advocate, Always an Advocate

Throughout my time as a state representative, I have learned time and again that the skills I used as an advocate to push for legislative change are just as important from the inside of the building as they are from outside. I can work to pass a policy, but in order to create long-lasting change, I also need to challenge long-held beliefs and assumptions. This means engaging in difficult conversations with those who oppose the policies I'm working on, because even if they don't support what I'm working on, maybe I can plant a seed that will eventually flower into a new way of thinking. At the end of the day, though, there are some people who will never change their views, so it is critical that we elect women who share our values into positions of power.

As a state representative, when I am presented with an issue, my go-to is to meet with advocates who work in that space. I want to understand what they're seeing in the field and work together to develop a policy solution and advocacy strategy. As someone now "on the inside," I can assist in speaking with my colleagues, talking through the committee process, sharing my knowledge of various state agencies, boards, working groups, and commissions, and help contextualize the issue in light of other pressing concerns.

For example, when working with advocates to see if Medicaid can cover diapers, I advised them to present their research on diaper needs and the impact of diaper insecurity to the Women and Children's Health Subcommittee of the legislature's Medicaid oversight body. This presentation got them before important decision-makers and brought public attention to the issue.

Another example was when I worked with those advocating for more equitable Medicaid reimbursement rates to ensure people have access to the healthcare they need. I connected that issue to the larger discussion of the healthcare workforce and how low reimbursement rates make it hard to recruit and retain workers.

There are all types of elected officials and all types of advocates, so not everyone will work in the same way. But, rather than seeing the relationship as one-directional, i.e. providing information to a legislator, it's important to see legislators as potential partners and allies in the work. After all, they weren't always an elected official. They were drawn to run for office for some reason or reasons. Getting to know them and then partnering with them is an important piece of your advocacy.

In much of the work I focus on, there are difficult conversations to be had. Talking about human trafficking, abortion, and sexual assault can be uncomfortable. But, giving people space to have those conversations is how we create change. When someone feels comfortable discussing the uncomfortable, you can help them see an issue from a different perspective. This takes a lot of patience and listening. We were all raised in this culture, and everyone brings with them their own baggage.

If we want to be able to move forward and improve conditions for women and girls, then we need to be able to give space for people to ask the hard questions or share their views, including their lived experiences, personal beliefs, and, yes, their biases. Some of those things can be hard to hear, especially when in opposition to where you stand. Having a network of people you trust who you can debrief and laugh with comes in really handy.

There will always be people who don't agree with you and people who like the status quo. Patriarchy benefits many people, and when you're working to shift the power imbalance there will be people who push back and stand in your way. This is why we must elect more women into positions of power. During one of my early women's studies classes in college, we learned about all the various types of feminism. While I love the idea of a revolution and creating a whole new society that values all people, my feminist approach is working to change the systems from the inside out. And, in order to do that, we need more women on the inside working to change those systems.

As more women are elected to positions of power, we need to challenge male ways of leading. I'd love to see us move away from dealmaking and power plays. It feels like politics today are like the Red Sox versus Yankees rivalry, except that it is the American people who lose, not a team. Women bring different leadership skills to positions of power. It's important that we lift those skills up rather than attempt to fit women into a male idea of power. I think that individually, it starts with knowing you're enough and being willing to ask questions when you need help. There is no need to pretend you know everything. At best it's annoying, and at worst, it can prevent you from learning and doing the best you can to improve conditions.

As more women are elected into positions of power, we see the issues being addressed at state legislatures changing as well. Imagine what that would look like in the federal government! Once we elected more women into the Connecticut General Assembly, we passed the Paid Family and

Medical Leave Act, an increase in the minimum wage, and changed our domestic violence laws.

Women aren't a monolith, however. We were all raised in a heteronormative, sexist, and racist culture, and not all women will raise other women up. Throughout history, and still today, there are women who have internalized misogyny and who benefit from the dominant, white patriarchal society, as evidenced by the conservative women leading the charge to ban abortion. While I firmly believe that we need more women in positions of power, I also feel just as strongly that we don't need the women who will continue to perpetuate white male systems of power.

In large part, that is why my colleagues and I formed the Women Supporting Women Political Action Committee in 2022. Our mission is to help elect pro-choice Democratic women into office at the state and local level. In addition to financial support, our goal is to provide a network of women who can help each other navigate systems that were created by and for men.

Two years ago, I formed the Endometriosis Working Group at the legislature. I've gained national attention for this work because it is the first of its kind in the country. Endometriosis impacts one in ten individuals with a uterus, but because it disproportionately impacts women it has been under-researched, and not taught in medical schools. On average, women go through a decade being misdiagnosed and told that the pain they're experiencing is in their head. It took women sharing their stories and women in leadership to finally bring this to the forefront.

Since forming the Working Group, we have raised awareness in Connecticut, passed legislation to establish a biorepository that can help researchers develop diagnostic tools and treatment, and we're looking to use our power to push for federal changes. Staying true to my beliefs, I used my position in power to elevate an issue that has been ignored for far too long and has caused far too many women immeasurable pain and suffering. Just think what more we can do with more women in office!

This brings me to what might be my final point (for now). Bring other women with you! Since my first days at NAR-AL Pro-Choice Connecticut, I have worked with interns. It wasn't easy at first. I had to learn how to share my time and how to delegate work. But, after years of learning on my part, I've had the privilege of working with so many women who have gone on to do amazing things all across the country. Share what you've learned. Open opportunities for other women. Lift each other up. One of the biggest gifts of my work has been creating (what feels like to me) a team of feminist advocates who are working to create amazing change.

I don't know what role might come next for me, but I do know that whatever it is, I will be advocating to make this country better for women and girls. These are interesting times, and while I in no way want to rush through this precious time I have, I am intrigued to see what future history books will include regarding recent years.

Power-hungry Republicans influenced by religious zealots are holding women hostage from obtaining abortion and causing maternal health to plummet, all while not doing anything to increase wages, lower housing costs, or improve healthcare. We are witnessing these same extremists ban books and school curricula, including women's, LGBTQIA+, and African American studies. You don't have to look far to see sexism, misogyny, and white supremacy at play. We are fighting back.

Effecting change is a long game, and the work is never done. So, give yourself the space you need, take a deep breath, and then get back in there. We need you.

Lessons Learned:

- Before meeting with an elected official, do research about what policies they've worked on or what their professional background is. Choose an issue you'd like to meet with an elected official on. Where can that research be conducted? What will you do with that research to help craft your message? Now make that appointment and have the meeting!

- Do you think women lead differently than men? How so? What are some perspectives they bring to the table that tend to differ from the most common approach men in leadership take right now?

- Make a list of local female leaders. How many women serve in your state legislature? In your town government? Of those women, which support your views? How can you support them in office?

Resources

Chapter 1 Resources

- In 1990, Connecticut state law was amended to read, "the decision to terminate a pregnancy prior to the viability of the fetus shall be solely that of the pregnant woman in consultation with her physician", the first such law in state codifying the Court's holding in *Roe v. Wade*, (https://reproductiverights.org/maps/state/connecticut/)

- Women also made great strides in politics in the 1990s. In 1992, dubbed "The Year of the Woman" by the news media, four women were elected to the Senate—Barbara Boxer and Dianne Feinstein of California, Carol Moseley Braun of Illinois (the first Black woman elected to the Senate), and Patty Murray of Washington—and 24 were elected to the House of Representatives. A year later, Janet Reno became the first woman to serve as U.S. attorney general.

- Erin El Issa, "Women and Credit Through the Decades: The 1990s," *Nerdwallet*, May 31, 2023.

- In 1992, with *Planned Parenthood v. Casey*, the Supreme Court reaffirmed the validity of a woman's right to abortion under *Roe v. Wade*. The case successfully challenged Pennsylvania's 1989 Abortion Control Act, which sought to reinstate restrictions previously ruled unconstitutional.

    ○ (https://www.infoplease.com/history/womens -history/timeline-us-womens-rights-1980-prese nt)

- The Violence Against Women Act tightens federal penalties for sex offenders, funds services for victims of rape and domestic violence, and provides for special training of police officers.

    ○ (https://www.infoplease.com/history/womens -history/timeline-us-womens-rights-1980-prese nt)

Chapter 2 Resources

- The revision of laws that had previously exempted rape in marriage began in Nebraska in 1976, and was not completed until 1993 in North Carolina. In Washington State, Seattle Rape Relief, formed in 1972, was one of the first rape crisis centers in the country, along with centers in Washington, D.C. and San Francisco.

- Near the end of the 1970s, activists held the first events that came to be known as Take Back the Night rallies.

- Rape crisis centers in cities and towns began joining together to form state and national coalitions. The Washington Coalition of Sexual Assault Programs was incorporated in 1979 with ten members from around the state. They had been working together to make legislative change, and to mark what was then Rape Awareness Week (now Sexual Assault Awareness Month).

- The National Coalition Against Sexual Assault (NCASA) was established in 1978, and one of its first conferences was held in Washington in 1982.

- (https://www.wcsap.org/advocacy/program-m
  anagement/new-directors/history/history-mov
  ement)

- **Women's Rights National Historical Park** was
  established in 1980, and covers a total of 6.83 acres
  (27,600 m^2) of land in Seneca Falls and nearby Wa-
  terloo, New York, United States.

  - (https://en.wikipedia.org/wiki/Women%27s
    Rights National Historical Park)

Chapter 3 Resources

- Christine Stuart, "Compassionate Care Bill Passes
  House 113 to 36," *CT News Junkie*, May 2, 2007.

  - https://ctnewsjunkie.com/2007/05/02/compa
    ssionate care bill passes house 113 to 36/)

- "Emergency Contraception for Rape Survivors,"
  Center for Reproductive Rights, November 1,
  2007.

  - (https://reproductiverights.org/emergency-con
    traception-for-rape-survivors/) Links to articles
    on Connecticut's passage of Plan B.

Chapter 4 Resources

- Beth Frerking, "NARAL Reeling from Obama Endorsement." *Politico*, May 16, 2008.

  ○ (https://www.politico.com/story/2008/05/naral-reeling-from-obama-endorsement-010408)

- Robert Pear, "Passions Flare as House Debates Birth Control Rule," The New York Times, February 16, 2012.

  ○ (https://www.nytimes.com/2012/02/17/us/politics/birth-control-coverage-rule-debated-at-house-hearing.html)

- Issue briefs: "How the Affordable Care Act Has Helped Women Gain Insurance and Improved Their Ability to Get Health Care," *The Commonwealth Fund*, August 10, 2017.

  ○ (https://www.commonwealthfund.org/publications/issue-briefs/2017/aug/how-affordable-care-act-has-helped-women-gain-insurance-and)

- Joanne D. Rosen, "The Public Health Risks of Crisis Pregnancy Centers," *The Guttmacher Institute*, Volume 44, Issue 3, pages 201-205, September 10, 2012.

  - (https://www.guttmacher.org/journals/psrh/2012/09/public-health-risks-crisis-pregnancy-centers)

Chapter 6 Resources

- "Women's Suffrage," *History.com*, October 29, 2009.

  - (https://www.history.com/topics/womens-history/the-fight-for-womens-suffrage)

- This Day in History series: "Equal Rights Amendment," March 22, 2024, *History.com*.

  - (https://www.history.com/this-day-in-history/equal-rights-amendment-passed-by-congress)

- "Black Women, Sexual Assault, and Criminalization," *National Black Women's Justice Institute*, April 11, 2023.

  - (https://www.nbwji.org/post/black-women-se

xual-assault-criminalization)

- Black Women and Girls: Sex Trafficking in the U.S.

  - (https://www.cbcfinc.org/wp-content/uploads/2020/05/SexTraffickingReport3.pdf)

- Feminista Jones, "Why Black Women Struggle More with Domestic Violence," *Time*, September 10, 2014.

  - (https://time.com/3313343/ray-rice-black-women-domestic-violence/)

- Linda Villarosa, "The Long Shadow of Eugenics in America," *The New York Times Magazine*, June 8, 2022.

  - (https://www.nytimes.com/2022/06/08/magazine/eugenics-movement-america.html)

Chapter 7 Resources

- "Resources on Running for Office," National Council on Independent Living.

  - (https://ncil.org/run-for-office/)

- Keith M. Phaneuf, "New Study: CT's Citizens'

Election Program Has Become a National Model for Clean Elections," *CT Mirror*, September 14, 2020.

- (https://ctmirror.org/2020/09/14/new-study -cts-citizens-elections-program-has-become-a-n ational-model-for-clean-elections/)

• Mikaela Porter, "As Aug. 14 Primary Approaches, Andy Fleischmann and Jillian Gilchrest Hit the Campaign Trail in West Hartford," *Hartford Courant*, August 6, 2018.

- (https://www.courant.com/2018/08/06/as-au g-14-primary-approaches-andy-fleischmann-an d-jillian-gilchrest-hit-the-campaign-trail-in-wes t-hartford/)

• Mikaela Porter, "Jillian Gilchrest Unseated A 12-Term Incumbent in West Hartford. Here's How She Did It," *Hartford Courant*, August 15, 2018.

- (https://www.courant.com/2018/08/15/jillian -gilchrest-unseated-a-12-term-incumbent-in-w est-hartford-heres-how-she-did-it/)

Chapter 9 Resources

- Jillian Gilchrest, "In Support of a 35% Tax on Ammunition," *CT Mirror*, Op-Ed, March 13, 2020.

  - (https://ctmirror.org/2020/03/13/in-support -of-a-35-tax-on-ammunition/)

- Tom Kutsch, "Medicaid Will Soon Fund a Powerful Gun Violence Intervention," *The Trace*, August 19, 2021.

  - (https://www.thetrace.org/newsletter/medicai d-will-soon-fund-a-powerful-gun-violence-inte rvention/)

- Emilie Munson, "In Bid to License Nail Technicians, Legislator Goes Outside the Norm," *CT Post*, March 5, 2019.

  - (https://www.ctpost.com/politics/article/To-li cense-nail-techs-legislator-deploys-unusual-136 65671.php)

- "The Typology of Modern Slavery: Defining Sex and Labor Trafficking in the United States," *Polaris*, March 1, 2017.

○ (https://polarisproject.org/resources/the-typol
ogy-of-modern-slavery-defining-sex-and-labor-t
rafficking-in-the-united-states/)

Chapter 10 Resources

- State Representative Jillian Gilchrest's Official Statement on Photoshopped Image: *"The fist says, "Do not lube," a reference to sex. It is irresponsible to ignore men who fight for unregulated access to guns while spewing sexism and racism. We know that a majority of gun violence is directed at women and those committing gun violence often have a history of violence against women. Not to mention, the recent incidents of vigilante gun violence perpetrated by white men against Black protestors. I'm disgusted that a man would spend his time making or sharing a sexist image of me with a racist trope because he objects to my policy positions. I'm not surprised that I'm being targeted by men who feel threatened by me. But I will not stand by and accept deep-seated prejudice when Black men and women are being killed by the police and are disproportionately the victims of gun violence. As a politician, I expect opposition. I welcome a difference of opinion. But I refuse to tolerate sexism and racism. Our political discourse is increasingly being replaced by hate and violence and I don't accept that. None of us should accept that and we should be doing everything we can to change it."*

- Connecticut General Assembly Sexual Harassment Policy

    - (https://www.cga.ct.gov/olm/docs/Sexual%20 Harassment%20Policy%202018.pdf)

About the Author

Jillian Gilchrest, MSW was elected to represent the 18th District of West Hartford in the Connecticut General Assembly (CGA) in 2018.

Prior to becoming a state representative, Jillian served as the Director of Health Professional Outreach for the Connecticut Coalition Against Domestic Violence, Executive Director of NARAL Pro-Choice Connecticut, and Director of

JILLIAN GILCHREST, MSW

Policy and Communications for the Connecticut Alliance to End Sexual Violence. She has extensive experience advocating for women's health and safety, in particular influencing public policy at the CGA.

Jillian holds a Master of Social Work degree with a focus in Policy Practice from the University of Connecticut School of Social Work, where she has taught Political Advocacy.

Jillian currently teaches at two universities in Connecticut.

www.JillianGilchrest.com
https://www.facebook.com/jilchrest
https://www.instagram.com/jilchrest
https://www.tiktok.com/@jilchrest
https://www.youtube.com/@jilchrest

GREEN HEART
LIVING
— PRESS —

Our Mission: To make the world a more loving and peaceful place—one book at a time.

Green Heart Living Press publishes books in the genres of personal development/self-help, memoir, business/entrepreneurship, spiritual growth, and transformational leadership.

We are a woman-owned business based in Connecticut. We specialize in amplifying the voices of authors from communities that often find themselves marginalized. We believe that by sharing our stories, we break down stigma and prejudice, increase empathy and understanding, and make the world a more peaceful and compassionate place for all.

You can meet Green Heart authors on the Green Heart Living YouTube channel and the Green Heart Living Podcast.

www.ingramcontent.com/pod-product-compliance
Lightning Source LLC
Chambersburg PA
CBHW061155120626
46546CB00005B/2076